I Love to Tell the Story

PROCLAIMING
THE GOOD NEWS
WITH PASSION

JOHN ROBBINS

Published 2025 by Seed and Shepherd, Little Rock, Arkansas

First edition

Manufactured in the United States of America

ISBN 979-8-9995140-0-4 (softcover)

Editorial production by Liz Russell Solutions
Book design by Studio 2020

For my wife, Susan,
who has been my faithful partner,
constant supporter,
and greatest encourager
through all my years of ministry
in churches in Arkansas and Texas

Contents

Acknowledgments

I want to express my profound and sincere gratitude to T.T. Tyler Thompson, OD, for the time, energy, encouragement, and effort he gave me in making this book a reality. I am thankful God made him a part of my life at a time when I needed him most.

I am also incredibly appreciative of Liz Russell and her expertise in walking me patiently through all the steps necessary so that this book could finally be published. Her expertise and pleasant demeanor have been an invaluable gift to me.

Finally, I want to say a special word of thanks to the members of Pulaski Heights United Methodist Church and all the other congregations I have served in both Arkansas and Texas for your unwavering grace over many years.

Introduction

I have wanted to write a book since I was a little boy. But like a lot of things in my life, I never seemed to find the time or make the effort to do it. Part of my struggle was what to write about. There are more than enough books on pastoral leadership or church growth, so I knew the world didn't need another book like that from me. Then it dawned on me: I write a small book, almost every week, called a sermon. Why not compile a few of the thousands of sermons I have written, memorized, and preached into a cohesive form and publish them? As a result, my first book is in print.

Years ago, a sixth-grade boy attending confirmation classes came into my office. I was supposed to ask him about what he had learned over the last several months. Before I knew it, he was interviewing me. He asked, "Do you do a lot of studying, praying, and researching before you write your sermon?" I said, "Yes." He then asked, "Do you spend many hours every week writing it and memorizing it?" Again, I said, "Yes." Then his final statement almost knocked me to my knees. He exclaimed, "That means you write a term paper almost every week of your life!" In other words, I write a small book most weeks!

So if I spend all that time researching, studying, praying, and memorizing, maybe I've got a book or two in all those sermons that can be useful in someone's walk with Christ. As a result, I have my first set of sermons in print for others to read entitled *I Love to Tell the Story*.

I pray this book is a source of encouragement. I pray it informs you of the love, grace, mercy, and forgiveness of the God we know in and through Jesus Christ. I pray you will be grateful you read it!

I think sermons should be practical and applicable for everyone. I am not a great theologian, but I have dealt with people facing the challenges of faith and life for four decades. As a result, I have come to believe sermons are a great source of strength for those who hear and read them if they offer the good news of Jesus Christ in a relatable way. I pray I have done that over the years.

This book is divided into four sections. My intent in each section is to offer a practical sermon about faith and life and how we navigate our relationship with the one who loves us unconditionally and forever.

May this book be a blessing. I pray that it will be so!

—*John Robbins*

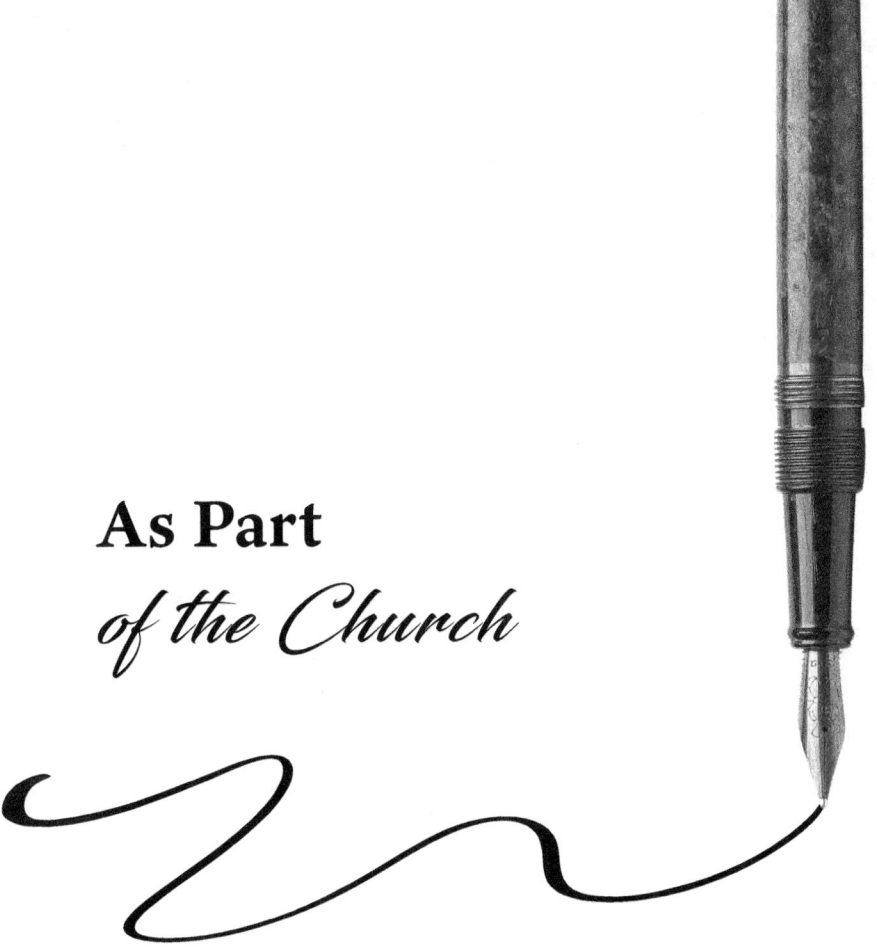

As Part
of the Church

Strength *through Weakness*

It is necessary to boast; nothing is to be gained by it, but I will go on to visions and revelations of the Lord. I know a person in Christ who fourteen years ago was caught up to the third heaven—whether in the body or out of the body I do not know; God knows. And I know that such a person—whether in the body or out of the body I do not know; God knows—was caught up into paradise and heard things that are not to be told, that no mortal is permitted to repeat. On behalf of such a one I will boast, but on my own behalf I will not boast, except of my weaknesses. But if I wish to boast, I will not be a fool, for I will be speaking the truth. But I refrain from it, so that no one may think better of me than what is seen in me or heard from me, even considering the exceptional character of the revelations. Therefore, to keep me from being too elated, a thorn was given me in the flesh, a messenger of Satan to torment me, to keep me from being too elated. Three times I appealed to the Lord about this, that it would leave me, but he said to me, "My grace is sufficient for you, for power is made perfect in weakness." So, I will boast all the more gladly of my weaknesses, so that the power of Christ may dwell in me. Therefore, I am content with weaknesses, insults, hardships, persecutions, and calamities for the sake of Christ, for whenever I am weak, then I am strong.

—2 CORINTHIANS 12:1–10

*N*o one was more loving, more forgiving, more grace-filled than Jesus Christ, and he was tortured, abandoned, and betrayed. He knew deep suffering.

No one tried to combat suffering more than Mother Teresa, but she lived a life as an adult most of the time extremely malnourished, incredibly lonely, and isolated. Desperate for love.

No one outside the apostle Paul did more to spread the good news of Jesus Christ in the early days of the church, but he was brutalized repeatedly. He was imprisoned time and again.

And even to this day, we know people—even maybe in our own families, certainly in our own communities—who, despite their extraordinary faith and their desire to be committed to Jesus Christ as best they can, are suffering in some way.

Sometimes suffering is our own fault. We suffer physically because we eat too much, smoke too often, drink way too much, never exercise, and have health issues as a result that can cause suffering. Relationally, we have caused our own suffering sometimes and the suffering of others, because we have been unfaithful and non-committed, breaking the trust of others, and now we live with that level of pain. But there are times in life when suffering is indiscriminate. It is inexplicable. The faithful and the unfaithful alike know pain and agony in all its many forms.

The apostle Paul wrote to the church at Corinth, concerned about those whom he referred to as "super apostles." They were the men who Paul believed were the kind of individuals who were elevating themselves above the gospel message and trying to belittle Paul and his authority in the process. So Paul said, "I'm going to take a moment to boast." And then he wrote in the third person about himself. "I knew a man who fourteen years ago was caught up to the third heaven." That meant the highest place. We don't believe in levels of heaven. What he meant by that was the highest state anyone can achieve in relationship with Almighty God.

And Paul said, "In that moment, what I experienced is something that was so profound and so great that I cannot even share it with you." But to appear humble, Paul spoke in the third person. But he was talking about himself. Then he said, "In order that I would not be too arrogant having had this extraordinary spiritual experience, I received a messenger from Satan. I have been afflicted. I have a thorn in my flesh." We don't know what the thorn is. There's no explanation ever in scripture of the kind of suffering Paul endured.

Now, we know he would have endured physical suffering because of all the stoning and other brutality that he experienced over the course of his ministry. Or was it something else? Was it spiritual? Was it relational? We don't know. But for whatever reason, Paul longed for whatever it was that was causing him such great suffering and torture to be removed from him. And he stated, "Three times"—most likely that means three periods in his life—"I went to God and asked for this to be removed from me. And each time God said, 'No. My grace is sufficient.'" In other words, live with it. Paul had to live with whatever it was that was causing him great suffering.

Then Paul said, "That's okay, because it is in my weakness, because of this suffering, that I truly find my strength, because I am now reliant on Jesus Christ more than myself to cope with whatever it is I am facing."

In her book *Gravity and Grace*, Simone Weil wrote, "The extreme greatness of Christianity lies in the fact that it does not seek a supernatural remedy for suffering, but a supernatural use for it."

Like the apostle Paul, many of us have experienced different levels of suffering in some form.

Scripture has never told us—nor does Christ in this moment when Paul spoke of him make the promise—that we will never suffer. The promise is that he will be with you in your suffering.

Remember even in the Gospel of John, Jesus said to his followers before he was crucified and resurrected, and before he ascended to the Father, "Those of you who follow me, get ready. It's going to hurt. You're going to suffer if you become a follower of mine."

There has never been a clearly defined explanation from God explaining why, as followers of Jesus Christ, we will not suffer. But we do. We all know good, faithful, committed people who have experienced a great deal of pain. And Paul says that when we go through that, it means that we have to be reliant on our relationship with Jesus Christ to be the ultimate strength to get us through whatever it is we are doing. Remember what Jesus said: "Apart from me, you can do nothing."

It is the understanding and the explanation that we need Jesus Christ that really, ironically, when we appear to be weakest, we are absolutely the strongest because we have that source greater than ourselves helping us, encouraging us, supporting us, and nurturing us when we would not have it otherwise.

In the fourth century, the Council of Nicaea met. There were 318 delegates. Only twelve of them had not lost an eye or a hand or limped significantly, having been tortured for their faith in Jesus Christ. We look at Jesus and Mother Teresa and the apostle Paul—these extraordinary figures that we recognize as having been so faithful, so committed, so loving, and so compassionate. And we remember how greatly they suffered in some form or other for the cause.

There is no clear explanation in scripture that says this is why you and I won't suffer. On the contrary, the promise is that we will suffer in some way, at some point in time in our lives. That is a part of the makeup of the faith. And that in the process of suffering, we will find a strength in our weakness to support us and encourage us and lift us up. What that means for all of us fundamentally is that we can't be self-reliant to such a degree that we don't need God.

For a lot of us, we think our charisma, our charm, our intellect, our good looks, whatever it may be, can carry us where we need to be through life. But then something happens beyond our control. The inexplicable takes place, and we ask the fundamental question, "Why, how can this happen?" There are things in life we all know that happen to every one of us that we don't anticipate or expect, much less welcome, but they happen anyway. And sometimes being completely self-reliant does us no good.

Sometimes life presents us with too much to bear. We can't handle it on our own. And we need one who is greater than us, who can give us the strength that sometimes we don't even understand to carry us through a situation or time in life that we could not manage on our own.

What happens when our health fails? Suddenly, we get that diagnosis. What do we do when seemingly overnight our good looks aren't going to have all the answers? Or our charm, our wit, or that previously dependable personality won't get us through a crisis? Or money won't solve the problem? On whom do we rely?

What happens when you get up to go to work for another day and before the day is out, your home is destroyed by a tornado? Your business is no more because trees have fallen on it? And family members or friends are injured or missing? What do we do? How do we cope?

Trying to do all of that completely alone is impossible. Somewhere along the way, eventually we are going to break down. But somewhere in all of that we discover that being a people who fundamentally believe that through that suffering, through that pain, there is a source greater than ourselves that undergirds us and holds us up and lifts us up so that we might somehow be strong enough to get through all of this.

Being weak does not mean being pitiful—not from the Christian perspective. Paul says, "I am strongest when I am weakest. When I am hurting, when I can't do it on my own, when my skill set doesn't measure up, when I am weak, that is when I am strong because I am completely reliant on a source greater than myself." We believe that to be true.

In fact, Paul saw suffering as a badge of honor because he believed in the one who suffered for him. So if he could suffer for Christ in return, Paul said, "I am ready. Bring it on."

Additionally, Paul stated, "I boast in my suffering because suffering produces perseverance, and perseverance produces character, and character produces hope, and hope does not disappoint us."

As a human being, I don't understand suffering. I mean, I don't get it. Why is it that oftentimes some of the most faithful, committed people we have ever known, who try and try and try, seemingly go through one trial of suffering after another? I have known some of the most faithful people in my entire life who never seem to catch a break.

It's not fair and it's not right, but it happens anyway.

I don't know why sometimes God seems to be so silent when we want God to shout, "It's going to be okay!" "God, where are you? I need you right now." I don't understand that. But what I do believe is that fundamentally in all of this, we need to be a people who tell ourselves time and time again, "I can do this *not* by myself, but because of the one in whom I put my trust, the one I rely on to be my source of hope and strength." That's certainly how Paul would have made it. Without that, we couldn't possibly make it on our own.

I read a biography some time ago about Susanna Wesley, the mother of John and Charles Wesley. John Wesley was the determined founder of the Methodist movement, and Charles Wesley wrote so many of the famous hymns that we sing Sunday after Sunday and at Christmas in our services of worship. Those two men were giants in the Christian faith, and she was mother to them both. Susanna Wesley also lost nine other children to death.

An extraordinarily faithful woman, she taught her children scripture every day, as well as the alphabet, by the time they started school, which happened to be in the Wesleys' home kitchen. Susanna Wesley was abandoned for a time by her own clergy husband, who became angry at her because she wouldn't show her allegiance to the king of England. She informed him that Christ is more important. So he left her with all those children she had to be responsible for.

Susanna Wesley was an extraordinarily lonely, isolated woman most of her adult life. You're not going to find a more faithful, committed mother and Christian, and yet she suffered so much. Doesn't seem to add up, does it? Doesn't make a lot of sense, but that's the way it was, because Susanna Wesley was one of those people, despite her circumstances, who was a believer that in all of that there was a source greater than herself to undergird her, to lift her up, and to encourage her along the way, and that was being in relationship with Jesus Christ. She found her strength in her weakness.

Remember what Jesus said: "I will never leave you nor forsake you." Under no circumstance are we alone. Even if we feel like it sometimes, the great promise to us is that we're never alone. We're never by ourselves. We don't have to do this thing called life alone.

Now, a lot of times we try, but every time we try, eventually, somehow along the way, we're going to fall flat. So like the apostle Paul, when we find ourselves in life dealing with whatever issues we must face (and by the way, all of us face issues), whatever they may be, who is your source of hope and strength to get through all of that?

When you feel alone or abandoned, somehow in all of that we need to remind ourselves that we are never in that condition, that we're going to get through this. We don't have to do it on our own. We can't do it on our own. Paul suffered greatly for the faith. When the book of Acts was written, it said in there when Paul became a follower of Jesus Christ, the resurrected Christ said, "I'm going to show him how much he is going to have to suffer for the faith." And suffer he did.

Paul was stoned repeatedly. One time he was stoned so severely that they thought he was dead. And they took him outside the city where he was revived, and he said, "Well, I'm going right back in." He was in prison time and again and was even bitten by a snake.

Paul was whipped repeatedly. Can you imagine what his body must have looked like, how scarred it was? You can only imagine what the prison conditions were in his day and time.

And he was in prison again and again. Now, how did he do all that? He didn't take a class on self-reliance. It wasn't his charisma and his charm. Certainly, it wasn't his good looks. It was a level of faith that enabled him to get through what he needed to get through. When he was weak, he was strong.

There's a story about a man stuck on an island by himself and in order to survive, he builds a little hut. Each night he sleeps in that hut, longing for the day when he'll be rescued. And one day he goes off into the distance to collect firewood and as he comes back, he discovers that his hut has been burned down. Somehow it caught fire and there's nothing left. Everything he relied on was gone, destroyed.

But soon afterward a ship arrived, and the captain of the ship told him, "I'm so glad that you lit a fire so we could see the smoke to know that there must be someone here to save."

It was only when everything that he was reliant upon was destroyed that he could be saved.

That within us is so self-reliant that whether we say it consciously to ourselves or not, we believe it to be so. "I can do this. I don't need your help." Somehow when we find ourselves in a situation where none of that works anymore, who is going to work on our behalf? Who's going to lift us up and encourage us? We believe and know it to be Jesus Christ.

So, if you feel weak, just remind yourself that in your weakness you are really very strong.

Hallelujah. Amen.

Slinging Seed

That same day Jesus went out of the house and sat beside the sea. Such great crowds gathered around him that he got into a boat and sat there, while the whole crowd stood on the beach. And he told them many things in parables, saying: "Listen! A sower went out to sow. And as he sowed, some seeds fell on a path, and the birds came and ate them up. Other seeds fell on rocky ground, where they did not have much soil, and they sprang up quickly, since they had no depth of soil. But when the sun rose, they were scorched, and since they had no root, they withered away. Other seeds fell among thorns, and the thorns grew up and choked them. Other seeds fell on good soil and brought forth grain, some a hundredfold, some sixty, some thirty. If you have ears, hear! When anyone hears the word of the kingdom and does not understand it, the evil one comes and snatches away what is sown in the heart; this is what was sown on the path. As for what was sown on rocky ground, this is the one who hears the word and immediately receives it with joy, yet such a person has no root but endures only for a while, and when trouble or persecution arises on account of the word, that person immediately falls away. As for what was sown among thorns, this is the one who hears the word, but the cares of this age and the lure of wealth choke the word, and it yields nothing. But as for what was sown on good soil, this is the one who hears the word and understands it, who indeed bears fruit and yields in one case a hundredfold, in another sixty, and in another thirty."

—Matthew 13:1–9, 19–23

*W*hen I was an undergraduate, I attended Tarleton State University in Stephenville, Texas, the rodeo capital of the world. Tarleton State has a huge school of agriculture, and people who live on large ranches and farms out in west Texas regularly attend TSU to be educated all the more about what it is they do on a ranch or a farm. I had friends who were agricultural education majors, agricultural business majors, and agricultural science majors. It was amazing to me how much science and math are involved in being a farmer.

Many of my friends would calculate all kinds of information that had to do with when it was the ideal time to place nutrients in the soil. What was the ideal amount? How much should be planted? What's going to happen if not enough is planted or too much is planted? Sometimes it is literally down to a matter of hours, the ideal time to plant, to reap, and to harvest. There is a lot that goes into being a farmer. Everything is detailed and structured a particular way.

Most of us take it for granted when we go to the grocery store that food items we want will be there. But for a lot of people on a daily basis, hard work and dedication are at least as much a part of the process for them providing for the rest of us what it is we enjoy so much.

A lot of science and a lot of math.

And then Jesus told a story about the most ridiculous of farmers. Irresponsible, wasteful, and reckless. This farmer has an abundance of seed. But he slings it everywhere, all over the place. There's no structure or order to it. There's no particular time frame. There's no statement about the best results. In fact, we learned from Jesus that this farmer slings seed into rocky ground where it never even takes root. Some of the seed is eaten quickly by the birds of the air. And some of the seed has a little depth and springs up, but it is quickly choked off because it's in thorns. But some of the seed actually takes root, and that seed produces an abundance, a huge harvest.

Now, more often than not, when Jesus told a parable in scripture, he just left the parable laying there. The listener must walk away thinking about what the parable meant. But in this instance, Jesus explained to us who the farmer was and what the seed was all about. We are those farmers. And it's on us, our responsibility to sow the seed.

Interestingly enough, we're supposed to sow it everywhere, sling it all over the place, make sure every corner, every crack and crevice has seed, knowing some of it will take root. But the vast majority of it, quite frankly, won't.

What Jesus is talking about in this parable is that we as people have a responsibility to share the good news of Jesus Christ, that seed with the world. We are the ones who have the obligation to make sure everybody, wherever they may be, has a chance to hear the good news. That's what evangelism is all about. That's what discipleship is all about. And Jesus makes it abundantly clear that the ones who have the mission to do it are his disciples, his followers. That's us.

Now, I want you to realize the emphasis that Jesus puts on the amount of seed that is not going to do much good, but that we should sling it anyway. In the life of the church, we spend a lot of time, energy, effort, and even money on our planting efforts. Sometimes it does great good and yields an extraordinary harvest. And other times, it doesn't do much good at all.

Why is that? Maybe, the timing wasn't right. Maybe the idea really wasn't what the respective church needed. Or maybe it just wasn't received well for whatever reason. But we all know that's how ministry works, not only in the life of the church, but in our own personal lives. Oftentimes, we can share what it means to be a follower of Jesus Christ in the simplest of ways—by how we go about living life. And sometimes, what we do and what we say takes root in someone else's life. They then notice who we are and what it is we say and how we go about interacting with each other. And it takes root in their life to such a degree that they want it for themselves. There's hopefully something compelling about who we are and the message we are trying to share with them.

But for others, they ignore the ministry we are offering altogether. It means nothing to them. It never takes root. Our challenge is to continue doing what we have been called to do individually and collectively as followers of Jesus Christ, knowing our role is to sling seed everywhere. That means in every circumstance and every situation in which we find ourselves, wherever we may be, we follow Jesus Christ. And we live in such a way that it becomes evident to everybody else. Then, somewhere along the way, even in those places we might think it would never take root, it might grab hold and produce an abundance, an overflow, an excess of ministerial harvest.

Anybody who's in the business of sales knows that oftentimes there's an inordinate amount of effort put into a project, and ultimately in the end there's no product or financial benefit. People in the real estate business or people who sell cars or people who still even today go door to door selling some kind of product, often find themselves spending a lot of time with a prospective customer with nothing to show for it in the end for the effort put forth. But those who believe in their product keep plugging away because there's eventually that one effort and that one time that makes all the difference in the world.

I used to play a lot of golf. I was a horrible golfer; I cheated every chance I got, doing whatever it took to trim my score. At the end of the day, they'd say, "John, what'd you shoot?" I'd say, "I shot a seventy-eight." Bemused, they'd respond, "Seventy-eight, really?" Defensively, I would counter, "Yeah, I shot a seventy-eight. What of it!?" I'd just go on into the nineteenth-hole bar, my mind already getting prepared to defend my arguable score for the next time we'd play the course.

But rarely, on a good day, when I was playing the links—about the time I was ready to chuck it all and say "I'm done with this; I can't stand this game. Whoever invented this was probably first cousin to Satan"—I would just walk up to the ball, hit it right down the fairway beautifully, or make a long putt when I wasn't even paying a lick of attention. And that one shot would carry me the rest of the time through all the bad stuff and into a glorious nineteenth-hole celebration.

We know what that's like in life. We're like that. The church is no different. We need to do a lot in the church to reap the benefits. We have got to spend a lot of money. We are required to put in a lot of time and energy and effort, sling seed all over the place in this community and across the world, hoping that at least part of it's going to take root. Jesus knew that. He experienced that himself. Now, think about Jesus. At the prime of his ministry, he was approximately thirty years old, and he opened up in his home church, if you will, the scroll of the prophet Isaiah and read that one is to come into the world who's going to cause the blind to see and the lame to walk—the anointed one. And Jesus then folded up the scroll and said, "That's me. I'm that guy." And you know what his hometown says? "You don't act like that." "Don't act like you're somebody special." "Don't do that!" They get so angry with him. So wound up with anger and spite, they try to throw him off a cliff. They probably didn't get an endorsement from his local church when he went to the committee to be considered for ordination. They probably just passed on by, but Jesus kept trying. And as he went about doing ministry, there were those who came up to him and said, "You're the prince of all demons!"

Jesus, who touched people and interacted with those others ignored and who made a huge difference in the world in so many ways, was accused of being the prince of all devils. But that didn't stop him. He kept slinging seed wherever he went. And then he said to his disciples, "Listen, I want you to go out into the community. I don't want you to take a purse with you. I don't want you to take any food. I want you to just start going out there, rely on the hospitality of those you interact with and share the good news." And then Jesus said, "But if they're unwilling to hear it, shake the dust off of your feet and move on." Jesus was keenly aware from personal experience and with interaction with the disciples that oftentimes the work they did in the name of Jesus Christ yielded nothing or very little.

But that's not what motivates us. What motivates us is that when it does take root, it produces a hundred-, fifty-, thirty-fold, and we keep plugging away. That's the good news about what it means to be a follower of Jesus Christ. We have the greatest news on Planet Earth, the greatest news any human being could ever hear, and it's our role to share it. Sometimes we say it explicitly. "Do you know Jesus Christ? Let me tell you about him." Other times, we share it just by how we interact with other people or the decisions we make as followers of our Lord.

A few years ago, Susan and I were in London, England on a tour, and we were in a taxi with a couple of other United Methodist pastors. We were driving from wherever we'd been sightseeing on our way back to the hotel, and we had to go through Trafalgar Square and all these other places along the way to get back. While in the taxi, we were in conversation with the cab driver, a really nice guy, when one of the other pastors, Patti, asked him, "Are you familiar with the Alpha program, that evangelism program?" And she could have been speaking Greek to the cab driver. He had no earthly idea about what he was being questioned. He laughed and said, "I don't go to church and don't know what you're talking about. An Alpha program? It's beans to me." And Patti went on and on, "It's this international program that brings people to Jesus Christ. It started in London right there at that church we passed. That's why I bring it up. But it's now worldwide," and she just went on and on, and I became pretty put out with her. I said, "Stop. He doesn't care." And she said, "John, how do you know he doesn't care unless I talk to him about it? And you never know." Then she commented, "I cannot go to sleep tonight if I pass by a church where that program started and I don't tell somebody else about it."

You know what she was doing? She was slinging seed all over the inside of a taxi, hoping that some of it would land in the driver's seat and take root. We unashamedly, unabashedly follow Jesus Christ. And you all know that in the world in which we live today—and I know every single generation has said it and had a right to say it—but I'm telling you all, we are at a time in history where if we turn away from Jesus much longer, there is no turning back. We have got to share the good news of Jesus Christ with the world. More and more problems are emerging in our world that are so much bigger than any of us could have ever anticipated. And the final answer to all of this is Jesus, I promise you, and it's on us to do it. So, we sling the good news everywhere. We can be dejected and frustrated and say, "I keep slinging it. I keep telling family members about Jesus. I keep telling coworkers. I keep trying to live the right way. It's doing absolutely no good." You don't know that. Somewhere along the way, it's taking root.

Your job is just slinging, and then to not worry about it from then on. God will take care of the rest. Jesus reminds us, listen, a lot of it's just not going to take root, but that doesn't stop you. You're a Christian farmer slinging it all over the place. Paul said, "I'm not ashamed of the gospel."

We can never live in such a way that we appear to be ashamed to follow Jesus Christ. We never keep quiet about this message. If you had a cure for cancer, would you keep that to yourself? Of course not. You would go to scientists right away and say, "I've got the formula to save millions of lives. Here it is." You would never keep that to yourself. If you had the capacity to feed every starving person on Planet Earth, you would never keep that capability to yourself. You would distribute whatever it is to make sure everybody had something to eat. We have the most important message for people who are lost, for people who are walking in darkness, for people who do not know the saving grace of Jesus Christ. Why would we ever keep that to ourselves? It is the most important message any human being can ever hear.

Jesus interacted with all kinds of folk. He interacted with children, the ostracized, the alienated, the outcast, the elite. He spoke with women publicly in a culture and at a time where that was forbidden. It was uncouth, inappropriate. He ate with tax collectors and sinners. Sinners by definition in the Bible were those people whose sins were exposed. They were not allowed to be a part of corporate worship because they were so sinful. Man, I'm glad that doesn't apply to us today because I wouldn't be standing in any pulpit.

Jesus interacted with all kinds of people, and sometimes his interaction created a change in the life of individuals and sometimes it didn't. He had lots of discussions with lots of folks during his ministry, including the judgmental Pharisees and the religious establishment! And look where that got him! Into such hot water that he ended up being crucified.

Nevertheless, we sling the seed anyway because Jesus did, because he told us to. We sling it all over the place on top of rocks, on top of mountains, in the trees, on the sidewalk, in the yard, wherever it may be. We don't worry about the science or the math of it. We just do it because some of it, somewhere along the way, whether we are aware of it or not, has taken root and is going to make a difference in the life of someone else. Henry David Thoreau said, "I have great faith in a seed. Convince me that you have a seed there, and I am prepared to expect wonders."

The culture in which we live today has been the way it is for a long time now, and that is true for the vast majority of people in our communities. For them, Sunday morning is no different from any other day of the week; it's just not. They go to soccer, and they go to softball and baseball. They go to gymnastic tournaments, and they go boating. And there's nothing wrong with those things. But oftentimes, people use those as an excuse never to engage in the life of the church. They're just too busy walking in darkness and don't even know it.

I'm talking about the kind of people who never think about the church, never think about the faith, and it never crosses their mind that they ought to give their lives to the one who gave his life for them. There are very affluent people, who have at face value anything and everything that the rest of us would ever want. Yet they are walking in darkness with unpleasant lives, deep down inside wanting to cry all the time. I know people like that, and you do too. So we sling seed all around them.

Is seed like that going to take root? We don't know, but we hope and pray it does. God will take care of that. Our job is to keep plugging away. Throw it all over the place. Be reckless with it to make sure that not one inch of any space doesn't have a chance to hear the good news of Jesus Christ.

I love the story of the famous violinist Fritz Kreisler. He wanted a beautiful, priceless violin, and he found a collector who had one such violin. They tried to work out a deal. He finally realized it wasn't going to happen. The collector wanted just too much money. Fritz Kreisler became dejected and brokenhearted because this had been a dream of his. But before he left the collector, Kreisler asked the gentleman, "Could I at least just play the violin for a few moments?" He was granted permission, and as he started to play, the collector started to cry. And when Fritz Kreisler finished playing, the collector said to him, "I have no right to keep this beautiful instrument. Take it to the world and let them hear. It's yours."

Now, you all, we have no right to keep this message to ourselves. We take it to the world to let them hear. Thank God for those farmers out there who take science seriously to provide food for us, who know when to plant, when to reap, when to harvest. They know how much soil in which to plant, the percentage of nutrients necessary for the soil, and all those kinds of things. Thank God for those people.

But we're farmers too. We just have a different kind of seed, and we're reckless about it, unashamedly so. We throw it all over the place in every situation, every day. We get frustrated sometimes, because it doesn't seem to be doing much good. We get tired of doing it sometimes. But it's who we are, and it's what we do. We sow the seeds of life and grace and mercy and love and forgiveness to the world in the name of Jesus Christ. And if we do our part and everybody else has a chance to do her or his part, this will be a different place we call our Planet Earth.

We have the greatest message, the most important message, the eternal message. And the world, whether they think so or not, needs to hear it. There is no one and nothing else as important as this message, and it's on us.

So we sling it everywhere. We sow the seed.
God will do the rest. We do our part.

Hallelujah. Amen.

No Longer *Divided*

> *Now before faith came, we were imprisoned and guarded under the law until faith would be revealed. Therefore the law was our disciplinarian until Christ came, so that we might be reckoned as righteous by faith. But now that faith has come, we are no longer subject to a disciplinarian, for in Christ Jesus you are all children of God through faith. As many of you as were baptized into Christ have clothed yourselves with Christ. There is no longer Jew or Greek; there is no longer slave or free; there is no longer male and female, for all of you are one in Christ Jesus. And if you belong to Christ, then you are Abraham's offspring, heirs according to the promise.*
>
> —GALATIANS 3:23–29

When I was in high school, I had a very special friend. He was a good friend of mine, but he was incredibly awkward. He was overweight. He suffered from acne. He was one of those people who dressed disheveled all the time. He wanted so desperately to fit in that oftentimes he would say the most inappropriate things. He was made fun of continually at school. He was laughed at. He was bullied.

He really had a tough time in his teen years. But he was a friend of mine. And the reason that he was a friend of mine had nothing to do with school, because we didn't even attend the same high school. It had everything to do with the church. Because my friend, who was so awkward, who said the most unappealing of things sometimes trying to fit in and to be cool, who suffered so terribly bad from acne, and who was made fun of repeatedly, was president of our youth group.

He was the one who had a place in the church. As much as he was made fun of at school and laughed at, he was president of the youth group at church. That's where he fit in. That's where he was somebody. That's where people didn't care if he had acne or dressed in such a disheveled sort of way. And it was amazing to me that when he fit in at the church, he didn't say those most inappropriate of things trying to fit in. Because he already did.

I have always appreciated the church over the years and how often those who sometimes have such a difficult path out in the world find their place in the church. They are somebody in the church when the world repeatedly tells them they are nobody.

A long time ago, Paul wrote to the church in Galatia. Paul was having to deal with people who were coming from every direction, former pagans and former Jews or people who were still Jews, who now believed that one of their very own was indeed the Savior of the world, Jesus Christ. People with all kinds of backgrounds were gathering together to worship.

What Paul had to do was find a way to unite these people so that they understood that they were no longer divided by those things in the world that oftentimes compartmentalized folks or labeled or categorized them.

So Paul said that those of us in the church were no longer Jew or Gentile. We were no longer slave or free, no longer male or female. We were and are one in Christ Jesus.

We are in a place where we as Christians have found ourselves in a position where we act oftentimes like the world acts. We now label people, and we compartmentalize people, and we categorize people. And if, for whatever reason, they are not in complete agreement with us, then we sometimes feel that we have every right to vilify them however we choose online, on television, in person, whatever it may be.

And I think one of the things that we as the church of Jesus Christ must do now is go back and look at the very beginning and say, "How did the church originally survive when it included so many different people coming from so many different directions, so many different backgrounds?" They were dependent on a handful of people to tell them who they should be. In this instance, it was the apostle Paul called by Jesus Christ himself who said to them, "We are no longer going to categorize you, male or female, Jew or Gentile, slave or free." Now, think about that. Out in the world, you and I are enslaved, but in the church, we're free. Can you imagine the problems created as a result?

Because we all live in the world we get caught up in categorizing and labeling and stereotyping and all those kinds of things. I'm as guilty as anybody else.

What we should do is remind ourselves that we are no longer divided by those things because Paul said we're one in Christ Jesus. So fundamentally, that means that our responsibility is to find those qualities and characteristics in every human being that are just like ours.

What draws us together? What makes us one in Christ Jesus? Well, if we really think about it, fundamentally, we are pretty much all the same. Now, the world says we're different. We have different skin color, different levels of education, different levels of income, different sexual orientations. We live in different neighborhoods. We have different occupations, different interests and hobbies and all those kinds of things. And sometimes those things define us. But when we gather together in the church, even with our different political points of view, we ought to be able ideally to sit down next to each other. You know why? Because we all believe in the same Jesus. He hasn't changed. If we can find a way in the life of the church to sit down together, worship together, learn together, fellowship together, we have accomplished something extraordinary. That means we are no longer divided. And that's what Paul wanted.

There are so many similarities between all of us. Every human being is created in the image of God. Every human being wants to love and be loved. Every human being wants to fit in and be somebody and have a sense of purpose and being in life. And every human being needs to be forgiven and is dependent on the grace of God. Every single one of us fits into those categories in so many ways. We are really alike.

So in the church, we are to be the ones who send the message to the world. You can be socially awkward, and you can have acne, and you have a place in church.

Eugene Peterson, who wrote what we know to be *The Message*, a paraphrase of the Bible, said, "The church is comprised of both mystery and mess." It always has been.

There's something mysterious that takes place when we gather together that is extraordinary in the midst of all the mess that we continue to make, even in the life of the church. So really, we need to find a way to clean up the mess.

I think one of the things that we have to do in the church universal (I'm talking about the whole church universal) is remind ourselves that we have the greatest message on Planet Earth, the most unifying message, and the most critical message that anybody could ever claim for herself or himself.

And yet we have allowed pettiness in the church. We have allowed the culture to step in and dictate how it is we talk to each other and how it is we define one another to such a degree that we have lost our place. We're losing our grip on the world as the church, in defining how we live. And we know how we should live. Ideally, we should live like Jesus lived.

But given the level of hypocrisy, which all of us can fall prey to, and the level of meanness and spitefulness and all those kinds of things that are now a part of the culture in which we live, we as a people who follow Jesus Christ have to remind ourselves that those outside the church are watching.

Why do so many people turn away from the church because of the staggering level of hypocrisy of people they see who worship on Sunday morning and then are so mean during the week? We are supposed to be a people who say to everybody in the world, you're somebody. You have a place. I don't always agree with you. I don't even always like you. But we love the same Lord, which means we have every right to be together and to work through those things

39

that are different from who we are, recognizing that there is more that connects us than there is that divides us.

What is important for us to remember is that if you look in biblical scripture, Jesus became most angry with hypocrites. In the twenty-third chapter of the Gospel of Matthew, Jesus said, "Woe to you, teachers of the law and Pharisees. You neglect the most like justice and mercy and righteousness" (Matthew 23:23).

He says, "You strain a gnat and swallow a camel." He's making a point. What we must remember, of course, is that our responsibility is to do our best to live like Jesus every single day in every situation. And we are going to fail, and we are going to have to be dependent on God's grace to pick us up and try again, and we're going to have to ask to be forgiven. But it is the effort that makes such a fundamental difference.

What Paul had to deal with is something that is very clear. He said, "Wait a minute, I know out in the world they're defining you in all these different ways, slave, free, male, female, Jew, Gentile, but when we gather together, we are one in Christ."

What can we do as the church of Jesus Christ to take that message out into the world and say, "We are one in humanity, all created in the image of God. We all bleed, we all cry, we all laugh, we are all the same fundamentally."

Why do we spend so much time looking at the differences in all of us when most of what we are about is just like everyone else? Jesus hung out with the lowliest of people and very influential people as well. His ministry was all about everybody. This one who was born in a manger also had the wise men with their expensive gifts bow down before him. He is an all-encompassing savior for the world to know, and it is on us to live in such a way that people long to know, what it is about us that is so different? What is it about us that is so compelling? What is it about us that they are drawn to? And we believe it is the power of the resurrected Christ living in and through us in such a way that we make a great difference in the world. And if the world needs to be different at any point in its history, it is right now.

So we try. We don't always get it right, but in the church, instead of looking at the things that people want to make fun of about somebody else who comes in, or the awkward person, or the gay person, or the straight person, or the tall person or short person, or whatever it may be, let's look at the fact that they are a human being like the rest of us.

I remember reading a story that during the civil rights movement, a little girl went home and said, "Mommy, today I sat next to a Negro in school." And her mommy said, "Really? How was it?" She said, "Well, Mommy, both of us were so scared that we held hands all day together." Now, I love that. You know what we need to do as a church? We need to start holding hands, not only with each other, but we need to be holding hands with the world. Here you have two little girls in a civil rights movement era, where you are clearly defined and you are compartmentalized, who find a way to say, "That doesn't matter. We're two little ones who are scared, and we're going to cling to each other." We ought to be a people who in a lot of ways are scared in the world in which we live today, but we have the answer to rid us of all that causes us fear, angst, and uncertainty. But you've got to reach out and you've got to hold somebody's hand.

Paul said, "We are one in Christ Jesus." One. That means there's no difference.

And really, fundamentally, if you think about it, the one to whom we bow down and worship ought to be the greatest power in our life that causes us to see the world differently. We do that so we're not spending an inordinate amount of time on things that we can call out in someone else that are different and upsetting to us. So instead of lashing out or striking back, we find a way to find what it is that we have in common and who it is that we have it in common with. And in the life of the church, if nothing else, the one to whom we bow down is the one we have in common. Hear me. It is the same Jesus.

The church has wrestled with this since its inception, since its birth. We have all these different denominations because we can't get along. We have the Roman Catholic Church. We have the Greek Orthodox Church. We have the Protestant Church. We have all kinds of nondenominational churches. There are all kinds of differences in the church, different kinds of theologies, different kinds of ways of living out the faith. I get all that, but it's still the same Jesus, however it is we worship.

Paul said, "We are one in Christ Jesus." That means that Jesus ought to be the one who has such a powerful presence in our lives that we live in such a way that we emulate his life as best we can. And if we really do that, then the church can reinvigorate itself, be reenergized, and once again take hold of the world and say, "We have the answer. We have the hope. We have the opportunity to be unified as a people worldwide."

Years ago, I heard a United Methodist bishop whose jurisdiction covered Chicago, Illinois. In a sermon she said that the mayor of Chicago asked churches on the Friday before Memorial Day to show up in their respective neighborhoods and play games with the neighbors and have cookouts among other events. The church needed to step outside its doors and be a part of the community. And she said on that day before Memorial Day, when they were accustomed to all kinds of shootings, there was not one shooting in the entire city of Chicago on that Friday.

You know why? Because the church went out and said, "Look, we're all in this together. We're all the same. We're really no different." Suddenly people put down their guns. And surprisingly people started interacting with each other and, at least for a while, as short as it was, nobody was killed.

If we did that exponentially, if we did that for the world, if we did it in our own homes, if we did it in the life of the church, if we did it in our place of employment, what difference could we make? Maybe we need to reach out and hold each other's hand.

Paul said we are no longer divided. The world can tell you you're different, but when you come to be with us as the body of Christ, we're all the same. I am a sinner, and so are you. I am in need of forgiveness, and so are you. I am dependent on the grace of God, and so are you.

Every single one of us are reliant on the God we know in and through Jesus Christ to be our source of hope and strength. It is on us and up to us to do something with it and to take seriously what the early church did. As we learned, the early church would eventually thrive as a result of all kinds of different people getting together.

We wouldn't be here today had it not been for those people setting aside some of their differences—and they continued to have differences. We know that, but the fundamental truth is they recognized that out in the world, the world can tell you you're somebody different, but here we're really all pretty much the same—no longer divided.

Some years ago, I read a biography of Robert E. Lee. He was a fascinating man in a lot of ways, a very intelligent man. But he was often said to be on the wrong side of history. Shortly after the Civil War, he owned a big piece of property in Arlington, Virginia, now known as Arlington Cemetery—sacred ground.

Robert E. Lee routinely went to church on Sundays, and as was customary in his church after the war, the black residents had to sit in the balcony for worship. When it came time to receive communion, the white folk would come down, and if there were any elements left over, then the black congregation (mostly former slaves) would come downstairs and participate in communion. Everybody knew the rules. It was customary.

But on one particular Sunday when the white folk came down, a former male slave stepped from the balcony and came down and knelt at the communion rail. As you can imagine, people were aghast by this. "He doesn't know his place." "He doesn't know where he belongs." And so, all the good Christian white folk got up to leave.

But there was one person that came down and knelt next to this former slave. And they took communion together. Guess who it was? Robert E. Lee. Now, let me tell you about that. I don't know where you stand on all that kind of stuff. You'll have to work through that yourself. But he was on the wrong side of history, I'm telling you, the times being what they were. But what he was doing in his own way was saying to somebody, "We are no longer divided. We had a war, but that war is over, and we have a common savior, and that's what's most important."

Now, we have got to figure out, in the world in which we live today, how we can be who we are called to be more effectively and more efficiently and certainly more faithfully.

It is difficult for me to imagine what Paul had to deal with in the early church. Lots and lots of stuff, I'm sure. But enough people took him seriously, and enough people took their faith seriously, that the church became a fledgling institution with a definite foothold.

And it still exists to this day, because enough people have taken seriously the understanding that you can be a goofy teenager and be made fun of, but you can come into this place and still be president of the youth group.

I know out there somebody will try to compartmentalize you or categorize you in a certain way, but you can come into our church where we try to see you as one of us—all the same in God's eyes.

That's what we hope it means to be the church. That's who we are, and we are going to work and work and work at it. We all fail, but every one of us has got to do better. I speak for myself as much as I speak for anyone else. We have got to *do* better. We have got to *be* better.

And we're going to work at it, because we are the church of Jesus Christ—no longer divided.

Hallelujah. Amen.

Come *and See*

> *The next day, John again was standing with two of his disciples, and as he watched Jesus walk by, he exclaimed, "Look, here is the Lamb of God!" The two disciples heard him say this, and they followed Jesus. When Jesus turned and saw them following, he said to them, "What are you looking for?" They said to him, "Rabbi" (which translated means Teacher), "where are you staying?" He said to them, "Come and see." They came and saw where he was staying, and they remained with him that day. It was about four o'clock in the afternoon. One of the two who heard John speak and followed him was Andrew, Simon Peter's brother. He first found his brother Simon and said to him, "We have found the Messiah (which is translated Anointed)." He brought Simon to Jesus, who looked at him and said, "You are Simon son of John. You are to be called Cephas (which is translated Peter)."*
>
> —JOHN 1:35–42

Over my years in ministry, three congregations that I previously served have relocated. One of the churches moved because the interstate was widened and they had no other choice. Two other churches relocated their facilities because they needed more space.

One of those churches started the relocation process before I left. They would eventually move after I left, but we started the process while I was still the senior pastor. Several years went by—in fact, almost a decade—and Susan and I happened to be in that same town. We decided to go back and see not only the church where it had relocated but what had happened to the original church that I had served. It was on a square in a county-seat town that was wildly popular with tourists.

It was shocking to me. When we went to the old facility where I served, the sanctuary had been turned into a dance hall. And on the very spot where I used to preside at weddings, baptisms, and funerals, as well as lay hands on sixth graders through confirmation—in addition to conducting all the other events that took place in that very spot—there now stood a margarita machine.

It was an unusual feeling, to say the least, that that sanctuary had now become a honky-tonk. We went down the hall to what had been the family life center that we built while I was there. It was no longer a big gymnasium, a multiuse space. It was now a steakhouse. It was a restaurant. But we found that the church's cornerstone was still where we'd left it, with my name on it and the name of the church embedded into the wall on the exterior. That was strange.

But the most unusual eye-opener was going down the hall to the old church staff complex, particularly my old office. It was a large space. And when I walked in, my world came apart just for a moment, because my old office was now a lingerie store. And on the very spot where I had stacked all my reference Bibles, there were now piles of women's unmentionables. And *that* freaked me out!

When we were leaving, I told Susan, "I'm just having a hard time with this. All my memories, my recollections of all the sacred experiences in this place, it's just hard for me to deal with all this." And she said, "John, it's just a reminder that the church is not the building."

So if the church is not the building, what is it? Well, the church is a body of people who are broken and sinful, who are searching for an experience with the holy, whether they fully realize it or not, who want to be acknowledged, who want to be appreciated, who want to know that they can move on from their past failures and mistakes, and who want to celebrate the great joys and experiences in life with someone greater than themselves—the God we know through Jesus Christ. That's the church filled with folks with imperfections, mistake-prone people, people who have been hurt and wounded by life and, ironically, even by the church itself.

But there's a power that the church possesses that is like no other institution, the power of the Holy Spirit to accomplish great good and to achieve a great deal, even with the broken, sinful people that we are.

One day, John the Baptist had a group of people following him as they were walking around. John noticed Jesus nearby, and he called him the "Lamb of God." That piqued the curiosity of a lot of people. And there were those who approached Jesus and said, "Are you the one? We want to know, Rabbi." And Jesus's response was, "Come and see."

Later, Jesus encountered Andrew and his brother Peter. Andrew and Peter would go to Nathaniel, a friend, and say, "We have just met the anointed one. He's from Nazareth."

And Nathaniel said, "Is there anything good that can come out of Nazareth?" And their response was, "Come and see."

Those are the three words of invitation we need to express to the world as a part of the body of Christ: *Come and see.* Now we understand with the technologically advanced world in which we live today that "Come and see" means more now than just being physically present. "Come and see" means experiencing the sacred and holy and to be in the presence in some form with those around us who long to experience the same. And in a variety of ways, I think we live in a world today where people want to "Come and see" as we do.

We have all figured out if we live long enough that there will be times when we just don't get it right. Surely there is someone or something out there that can give us better direction and more hope than we are able to achieve on our own. We believe that to be the church of Jesus Christ. So come and see. If you're curious, come and see. That's what we ought to be saying to others because we are all a curious people.

We know that when there is any kind of a wreck on the highway there is a bottleneck. Why is there a bottleneck? Because there is a part of us that just wants to see what happened. We're curious about that. We're curious people because someone will come up to us and say, "Hey, you're not going to believe what I heard. Do you want to hear it?" "Yeah, of course I want to hear it." Good or bad? Salacious? It doesn't matter. We're curious.

That's the kind of people that we are. And we ought to build on the curiosity of other human beings by saying, "You ought to come to church." Well, what is it about the church? Is there anything good that can come from the church? Well, come and see.

The great joy of being a part of the body of Christ that we call the church is that you can be just who you are. There's no room in the church for pretense. Just come as you are. You don't have to have it all together. You don't have to be beautiful. You don't have to be eloquent. Just come and know that you will be loved, you are needed, and most importantly, you are wanted. The church is stronger when you are a part of the body of Christ and that much weaker when you're not.

Being a part of the life of the church allows us to be a part of something much bigger than ourselves by the power of the Holy Spirit. The great work that we do literally impacts not only this congregation, not only this community, but literally the ripple effect goes across the world. We do so much good for so many in many corners of the world because we believe that through the work we do we are empowered by the Holy Spirit to accomplish much. We believe that there is a greater source than us leading the way.

How does that happen? Well, come and see. Be a part of it. Involve yourself in some way and you'll find out. And sometimes we simply can't even articulate it. Things happen in the life of the church that are bigger than all of us and we don't get it. We don't know why it works so well, but it does. So come and see.

The primary way in which we experience the sacred and holy that we all long for, whether we fully understand it or even realize it, is through a worship experience. There's something that takes place, as mysterious as it is, in the life of the church that transforms and changes and reconnects and heals and educates and informs like nowhere else.

John Wesley, the founder of the Methodist movement, was a clergyman, and he struggled with his faith. He didn't even know if he was saved. He didn't even know if he really knew a relationship with Jesus Christ until a particular worship service that he reluctantly attended. And then his heart was strangely warmed.

The man who preached to more human beings than any other person in history, Billy Graham, was converted when he went to a revival reluctantly as a teenager. It was the worship experience that transformed his life, and he would preach to more than 215 million people in person and billions of people over the years on radio and television.

There's something that takes place through worship that can change us, that can make us whole. We don't always understand it, but the good news about being a part of the life of the church is, despite our imperfections and our failures and our shortcomings, we're always welcome. We are an inclusive community in a world of exclusivity.

Now, you think about it for a moment. Even our schools are exclusive. They must be at some level. Private schools obviously are exclusive. They cater to a particular group of people who can afford to go to a private school. Some can't, but those who can't afford it still have to live in a certain area, a certain district to attend a particular school. Schools have to be very exclusive, or you would have chaos, particularly in public schools. You live on one side of town, you don't go to school on the other side of town, you go to the school closest to you, that kind of thing.

We know that there are organizations that are based on age. You cannot join AARP if you're twenty-five years old. They're not going to have you. It's exclusive, fifty years old or older. If you're in Congress and you're a part of the Congressional Women's Caucus, if you're a man and you try to go in, you know what they're going to say? You're not welcome here. This is for women.

We live in a world where there are many exclusivities, but not in the life of the church. You can be a man; you can be a woman. You can be fifty; you can be twenty-five. You can have a job; you can be unemployed. You can be rich; you can live under a bridge. You can have multiple degrees hanging on your wall; you can never have made it through elementary school. It doesn't matter. We are the body of Christ.

And how does that work with so much diversity regarding age and gender, sexual orientation and race, and all these other things that cause us to be compartmentalized, but not in the church? How do we pull this off? Well, come and see.

Years ago, I was serving a church in that same community where they would eventually turn the sanctuary into a honky-tonk. There was a new doctor in town, and I was smitten to go see him. And the reason I was smitten to go see him was because he was a high school classmate of mine. I hadn't seen him in years, and now he was a doctor in town. I went to see him. He was taken aback by the fact that I would come see him, not because I would choose to see him but because of my profession. The first time I visited him, I cannot tell you how many times he said to me,

"Are you really a pastor?" "Are you kidding me?" "You're a pastor?" "Seriously, you're a pastor?"

And then I saw him numerous times after that. And every time I saw him, he would say to me, "What's going on in your church?" And I'd tell him. "Really?" he'd respond. "What else is going on in church?" "Who attends your church?" "What do you all do?" I mean, just time and time again, he'd questioned me.

And then one day when I went to see him, he said, "Hey, I joined a church." I said, "You joined another church? Why didn't you join my church?" He said, "Because you never invited me." He said, "Every time I asked you about your church, you told me what was going on, but you never asked me to visit." See, there were only three words I needed to say to him—and I never said them: "Come and see."

Now, I'm grateful that he joined a church, and I haven't seen him since I moved from that community. I hope he's doing well. I hope he's thriving in that congregation. But I missed a chance because I didn't say three simple words: "Come and see."

When we gather together, we remind ourselves of who we are and to whom it is we belong. The apostle Paul tells the church in Corinth, "You are not your own. You have been bought with a price." We're not really our own people. We belong to each other. And most importantly, we belong to God. And that's what it means to be a part of the life of the church. Well how does that work? We're so different in so many ways. Well, come and see. The church has been successfully doing that now for more than two thousand years.

I don't know how it all works. I don't know how we always accomplish what we accomplish. We don't always get along with each other. But somehow, some way, we do what we are fundamentally called to do because there is a power greater than ourselves we know to be God. And that's the God we know in and through Jesus Christ, the God of all creation and the God who empowers us by his Spirit to be who God would have us to be.

So come and see. Be a part of all of this.

Jesus walks by. People are curious. Lamb of God? Him? Yeah.

"Jesus, can we hang out with you today?" "Where you staying?"

"Well, come and see."

Three simple words with great power.

So this week, somewhere along the way, I promise you, you're going to have an opportunity to invite someone to be a part of your faith community. Don't be shy to ask them to come and see what's going on. Come and see where from their earliest days, children are taught that they are loved by God. Their earliest memories will always reflect of having been included.

That's why we invite children to come down to participate in the sacrament of Holy Communion. Many don't have any earthly idea what's going on, but I can tell you, a lot of adults have no idea what's going on either. But when the children come down, we do the same for them that we do for everyone else. You know why? We want their earliest memories to be that they've always been included. They've always been a part of the life of the church.

Come and see where you can be an awkward teenager with acne and uncomfortable and trying to figure out who you are and everything else, and then you come up here and you participate and you discover everybody else may be different at school, but there's something about being in the church that makes it okay to hang out with one another, and I can just be who I am. So come and see what that's all about.

We have divorced people. We have married people. We have single people. We have widowed people. We have people who are looking and searching for a relationship. We have others who have just come out of a relationship. So come and see. This is for you.

When I was in seminary, I used to wonder, why are there so many strange people? I mean, there are a lot of weird people that go to seminary. Why is that? And I've learned over the years why! Because a lot of strange people have been strange their whole life, and the one place where they can always be accepted, being a little bit different, was in the life of the church. And so many of those people didn't want to live a moment of their lives outside the church, so they gave their lives in service to the church, so they could always just be who they were. I love that. Come and see.

It's imperfect and full of folks like you and me. And by golly, we pull it off time and time again. How does that happen? I don't know. But come and see.

Hallelujah. Amen.

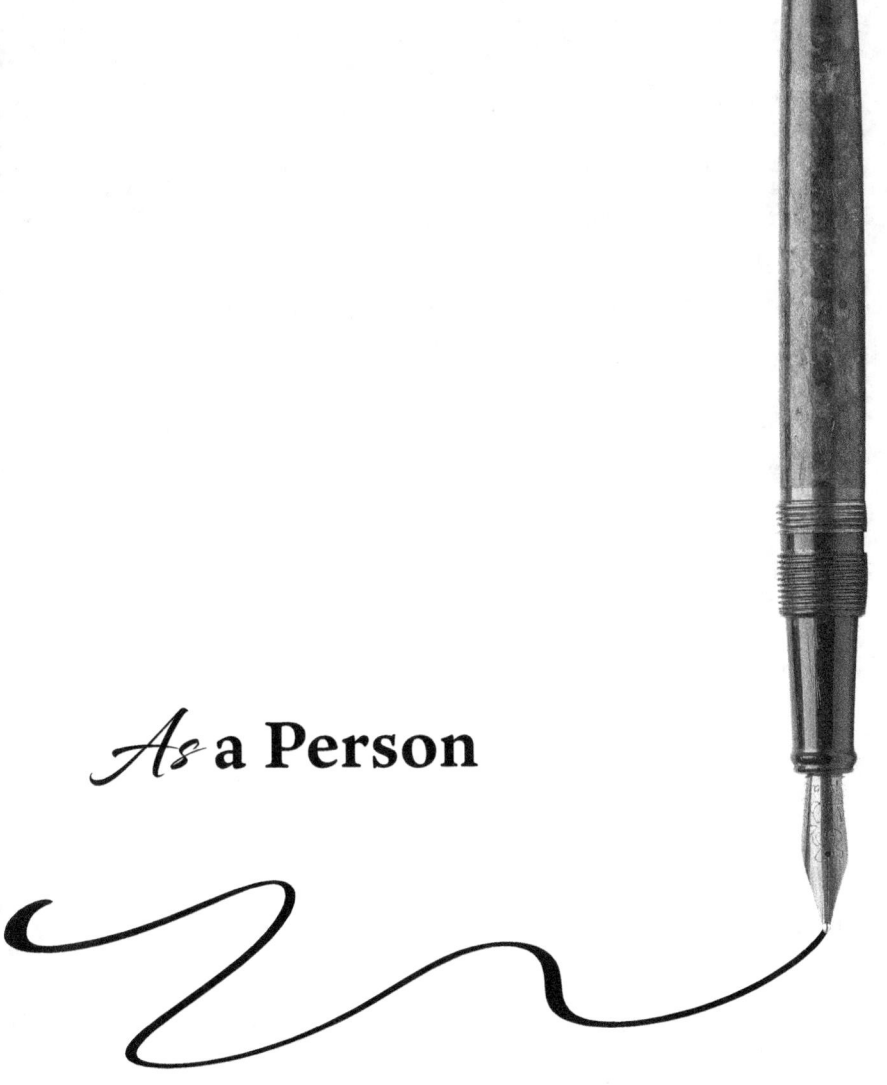

As **a Person**

My Life *Is My Witness*

> *Now the eleven disciples went to Galilee, to the mountain to which Jesus had directed them. When they saw him, they worshiped him, but they doubted. And Jesus came and said to them, "All authority in heaven and on earth has been given to me. Go therefore and make disciples of all nations, baptizing them in the name of the Father and of the Son and of the Holy Spirit and teaching them to obey everything that I have commanded you. And remember, I am with you always, to the end of the age."*
>
> —MATTHEW 28:16–20

*W*hen my dad was in junior high school, he had a Sunday school teacher by the name of Betty. Betty walked very awkwardly. There were only junior high boys in her class, because in those days they were segregated by gender. And those kids would make fun of Betty, mimicking her walk as she shifted from side to side, slowly shuffling her feet.

Betty also sweated a lot because in the early 1950s in their small church there was no air conditioning, causing her makeup to smear. They laughed at her behind her back and called her sweaty Betty. Betty's dress or skirt, whichever she happened to be wearing on any Sunday, was always terribly wrinkled and usually hung to her ankles. Betty didn't hear particularly well. But it was still funny to them to

59

make fun of Betty, sweaty Betty. But that would all change come one certain Sunday morning.

My dad describes how he and a couple of other junior high boys, for whatever reason, arrived early that Sunday morning. Betty was always there to greet them, the first teacher to show up. But on this Sunday, my dad and a couple of other boys were also there early. As they were making their way to the third floor where their Sunday school room was, they noticed something that would forever change their understanding of sweaty Betty.

As they were starting to ascend the stairs to the third floor, they realized that Betty was already making her way, crawling on her hands and knees up the flights of stairs. They realized that the reason Betty wore dresses or skirts to her ankles was to try to hide the leg braces on both of her legs. When you have leg braces, you walk awkwardly. As Betty was making her way, crawling hands and feet up each step, all the way to the third floor, they noticed that because it was so hot with no air conditioning and no elevator in the church, Betty began to sweat profusely. And that under those conditions, one is bound to sweat, and if you're a woman wearing makeup, it's going to smear.

And as they watched Betty, they realized that there was no wonder her dress got wrinkled, because when climbing steps on your hands and knees to get to the third floor to teach a bunch of unruly junior high boys about Jesus Christ you're bound to wrinkle your skirt or your dress just a little bit. And because Betty didn't hear particularly well, for whatever reason, she never noticed my dad and a couple of other boys watching her.

But that experience forever changed their view of Betty. There was no more mocking her, no more making fun of her behind her back, no more mimicking her awkward walk. Suddenly, this woman—who, they would find out later, had suffered from polio as a child—was like a saint to all of them. And if you talk to my father even to this day and you ask him, "Who is the most influential person in your life in your own faith development?" he is not going to say his parents, though they were very influential in his faith development. He's not going to talk about seminary professors that shaped his theology. He *is* going to talk about the quiet witness of a woman who crawled on her hands and knees every Sunday morning to share the good news of Jesus Christ with a bunch of junior high boys.

The quiet witness of Betty shaped the lives of a lot of boys who might not have ever understood who Jesus Christ was or is otherwise. But today, our witness is how we convey the message of Jesus Christ through our behavior, through our words, how we go about living daily in the mundane and the routine and the ordinary.

The clear definition of who we are, that is our witness to the faith. And we promise Jesus Christ and his church that we will be loyal in terms of how we live out our faith, by how it is we behave, and what it is we say. Jesus had been crucified and resurrected, but before he ascended to the Father, he offered what we know to be the Great Commission. "Go," he said, "all of you, and make disciples in the name of the Father and the Son and the Holy Spirit."

He said, "Go and make disciples and baptize and teach and obey." That is our witness if we follow our Lord and do what he asked us to do. And the primary way in which we go about making disciples is by who we are on a regular basis. It's on *us* to do that. It's not up to the government to tell others about Jesus Christ. It's not up to our schools to teach people about Jesus Christ. It is not the military's responsibility to threaten everybody into becoming followers of Jesus Christ. And the message of Jesus Christ will die if we do not do our part to be witnesses to the faith every day by who we are, being genuine and sincere followers of our Lord.

We are imperfect, we sin, we don't always get it right, but our responsibility is to do our best to make sure we live in such a way that, when people see us, they see our quiet witness. And they may say to themselves in some way or another, *There is something about her. There is something about him that is compelling, and I want to be like that.* Jesus said, "Go into all the world and make disciples." A disciple is simply an apprentice of the faith. Jesus also said, "Go out and teach so that more and more students can learn so that they themselves one day can be teachers of the faith." For the first four hundred years of the Christian movement there was no real great preacher, and yet Christianity would sweep across the Mediterranean world at a rapid pace because of the witness of the common everyday Christian.

It wasn't until John Chrysostom became Archbishop of Constantinople in the fourth century that people began to become followers of Jesus Christ because of preaching. Up until then it was the quiet witness of how people chose to live, and those on the outside looking in who thought, *There is something about this Christian faith that is so compelling, and I want to be like that.* And more and more people claimed the faith not because of a great orator but as the result of a common everyday life lived out in faith.

Now, there are always going to be those kinds of people who can quote scripture. I can quote scripture. You can quote scripture; just memorize it. It doesn't take any talent or skill to throw out a passage of scripture. I can do that all the time, and I have very little talent and very little skill. I can do that with the best of them. But just throwing out scripture does not make me a Christian.

And then you have those kinds of people who will come up to you and say when you're on the beach or somewhere else, "Hey listen, if you died today right now, would you go to heaven or go to hell?" And we want to say, "You go to hell and get out of the way. I'm having fun at the beach." It's a turnoff. That is not the way that we witness to the faith. That doesn't do much good. Maybe it does for a few, but for most of us, the way in which we go about being an example of Jesus Christ to the rest of the world is our witness.

I promise that I will live in such a way, as sinful as I am, to do my best to be an example to other people of what it means to live faithfully and loyally with integrity in my relationship with my Lord. That's the best witness that you can offer. If you can quote scripture, that is wonderful. That means you're reading your Bible, but don't use it as a tool for self-aggrandizement. Use it instead as a way of saying, "This is why I believe what I believe, and this is who I am, and why I behave the way I behave."

Not all of us are going to stand up and preach. I think about people like Billy Graham. He was unique. Billy Graham preached to more than 215 million people face-to-face, and if you count radio and television, many billions of people. The rest of us are not like Billy Graham, but our message, like his, can have a profound effect on people well beyond us. There is a ripple effect by the power of the Holy Spirit. Somehow when we live as we're called to live, it can influence others who may end up living as she or he is called to live, and then as a result it may affect someone else and someone else and someone else.

Most of us are not going to be great prolific Christian writers who sell millions of books like Beth Moore or Max Lucado. But the message we write with our life is fundamentally the kind of message that's possibly going to make a difference in the life of other people, whether you know it or not. They are reading you and formulating in their own mind an understanding of what it means to be a follower of Jesus Christ because you have the audacity to say that you do follow him.

For years, Charles Stanley preached on television across the United States and across the world. People from all over the world got to hear him preach every Sunday. Most of us don't preach to people all the way around the world, but our sermon is our life. And how do we articulate a message that we follow? We do it by how we behave, the decisions that we make. It is oftentimes a quiet witness. We are so involved in our relationship with our Lord that simply who we are is the message, the sermon in and of itself. Now, if you're given the opportunity to say to someone, "This is why I follow Jesus Christ," please do it. But the most powerful witness that you promised this church and God you would share is you living like Jesus.

Jesus gathered those handful of disciples—and it wouldn't have been just the eleven. Remember by this time

Judas had hanged himself. At this point it was just the eleven major disciples, the handpicked ones, but there were also a few other followers, and they were called disciples as well. And Jesus said to them, "You go out into the whole world, and you go make a bunch of other disciples." Now, that means of course that they wouldn't have had to tell people about Jesus. It means that fundamentally what Jesus is saying to them is, *Go into all the world. Your message now goes beyond the borders of Israel. The message now goes to the whole world, to the Gentiles, to everybody else.*

Everyone needs to hear the message of Jesus Christ, and I don't know one person that cannot benefit from hearing the good news of Jesus Christ. And you promised that you would live in such a way that you would share his message. It is about how we live, but it is also about what it is we say when we encounter other people on a continual basis or a one-time situation. What do we do? How do we live? What do we say?

They're watching whether you think so or not. I promise you they are watching, and some are ready to pounce on us and say, "I told you so. They're nothing but a bunch of hypocrites." But there are others, however, who look at all of this and say, "My gosh, what is it about her? There's something about her that's so attractive to me by how she lives, the way she interacts with other people, the decisions that she makes. I want to be more like that." That is that quiet witness that we promised we would offer up.

The New Testament is filled with examples of how people share the good news of Jesus Christ, often the kinds of people we would never choose. But their impact was and is so great. Think about the shepherds, the lowliest of all people. You have the shepherds and the narrative of the birth of Jesus Christ, and then at some point you have what we call the Magi, the wise men who encounter baby Jesus. The wise men, the smartest of all of them, leave quietly, the Bible says, after they encounter Jesus. But you know what the shepherds do? They go tell everybody. It's these lowly shepherds that get it right. It's the sophisticated, wealthy intellectuals who say nothing.

Here was John the Baptist who had this huge following. He was a charismatic personality with a baptism of repentance. His message was threatening, a "Get it right or go to hell" kind of thing. And then with all of those followers, he said, "I need to tell you something. There's one who's coming who's greater than I am. I'm not even worthy to untie his sandals." With all that attention, John turned the attention away from himself and put it on Jesus.

There was a woman who went to a well, because women went to the well. It was a menial task. Men didn't draw water from the well. Leave it to the women. And a woman went to the well, and lo and behold, there was Jesus. What's he doing at the well? He's going to have an encounter with this woman. She's been married five times. She's now living with someone who is not her husband. She's been passed off from one man to another. Remember, she didn't have the power to get a divorce, which means, of course, that her husbands used her, got rid of her. She went to another husband who used her, got rid of her, over and over. She is used up, if you will. And Jesus tells her about living water. She is the first person in recorded scripture to go out and tell anybody outside the Jewish community about Jesus Christ. And what that means is, she was the very first evangelist. A woman—a woman who didn't have a voice, a woman who was used up, a woman who was there just to draw water—became the first person to tell the rest of the world about Jesus.

And then you have Mary Magdalene. Scripture tells us Jesus had to cast numerous demons out of her. And in all four gospel accounts of the resurrection of Jesus Christ, Mary Magdalene was the one who said, "I have seen the Lord." You know what the disciples did? They went to the tomb, they looked around, and they went back. But Mary Magdalene actively proclaimed, "I've seen the Lord."

Oftentimes, there are those people who we would never anticipate being a voice for God but who live in such a way, speak in such a way, make decisions in such a way that the rest of us are compelled to follow the one they follow. And you said you promise to be that way.

My first year in seminary, I got a speeding ticket. It cost so much money, I decided, "I don't have any money anyway, I'll just take the optional defensive driving course." I had to spend a Saturday taking a defensive driving class in the lobby of a hotel—not in a ballroom, but in a run-down hotel lobby where they just set up some chairs in a circle. The facilitator came in and said, "If you stay here all day, you get a certificate you can give to your insurance company. You can show it to the judge, and your ticket will be dismissed." So I knew I was going to have to be there all day long.

As I sat there while we were going around the room introducing ourselves, the facilitator asked everybody to say what it was they did. Most of those in the room were eighteen-wheel truckers, and they looked like it. And here I was, this young, sweet, lanky, innocent seminary student. When it was my turn the facilitator said, "Tell us your name." I announced, "My name is John Robbins." And they said, "Well, what do you do?" I said, "I'm a graduate student." They said, "A graduate student? What are you studying?" And I just so quickly wanted to say law or economics or something else. But I said, "Oh, I'm studying to be a pastor." And they then went on to the person next to me who just opened up. "Let me just tell you. I've got a drug problem, and I have an alcohol problem. I got stopped by the police and this, that, and the other. And if I get one more ticket, I'm going to jail, and my life is a living mess." To which I wanted to say, "Dude, this is not a therapy session. Let's just get this over with. I don't want to be here. I just want to leave." But I didn't.

We eventually finished going around the room, until we did all we needed to do. By the last break of the day, I had done a masterful job of not talking to anybody the whole session. I went to the Coke machine to get a Coke, and this young man who'd been sitting next to me and thought it had been a therapy session walked up to me and said, "Hey, ain't you the guy that's going to seminary?" And I said, "Yes, I am." He calmly stated, "My life is really messed up. Would you tell me about Jesus?"

And I thought (now I'm being honest), I thought to myself, *How dare you? I'm trying to get a Coke. We've got ten more minutes of this thing and I'm out of here. I don't want to talk to you. I don't want to talk to anybody else.* And he said, "I got to do something with my life." And I just kind of hemmed and hawed for about thirty seconds until the facilitator said, "Y'all get back here." And Mr. I-Need-Therapy, almost begging, repeated, "Can I talk to you afterward?" I said, "Sure."

And I'm ashamed to admit it, but as soon as it was over, I got my certificate and left the building. I've never seen that young man since, and that's been almost forty years ago. But I have been on my knees begging God numerous times to forgive me for leaving him like that.

His life was so messed up and all he did was ask me, "Tell me why you follow this guy. I need that." And I had promised earlier. I had promised God that I would be a witness to the faith, and I failed miserably. I hope I've done better and *will* do better. I don't always get it right. I hope I'm doing better, and I hope you're doing better. We're just trying to be who we promised God and the church we would be, living that quiet witness. And when we have a chance to tell somebody about Jesus, shout it from the rooftops. It's who we are supposed to be. We are people who made a promise. Let's stick to it.

Hallelujah. Amen.

Taming the Tongue

> *Not many of you should become teachers, my brothers and sisters, for you know that we who teach will face stricter judgment. For all of us make many mistakes. Anyone who makes no mistakes in speaking is mature, able to keep the whole body in check with a bridle. If we put bits into the mouths of horses to make them obey us, we guide their whole bodies. Or look at ships: though they are so large and are driven by strong winds, yet they are guided by a very small rudder wherever the will of the pilot directs. So also, the tongue is a small member, yet it boasts of great exploits. How great a forest is set ablaze by such a small fire! And the tongue is a fire. The tongue is placed among our members as a world of iniquity; it stains the whole body, sets on fire the cycle of life, and is itself set on fire by hell. For every species of beast and bird, of reptile and sea creature, can be tamed and has been tamed by the human species, but no one can tame the tongue—a restless evil, full of deadly poison. With it we bless the Lord and Father, and with it we curse people, made in the likeness of God. From the same mouth comes a blessing and a curse.*
>
> —JAMES 3:1–10

I am not a horseman, but I do know that even the most powerful of horses can be directed in the way we choose with a bit and a bridle. I am not a sailor, but I do know that the greatest of ships can be turned by the smallest of rudders. I am not a psychologist, but I do know that the tongue, the words we speak, can leave a lasting imprint on the psyche of other people.

In the book of Proverbs there is a verse that states, "Death and life are in the power of the tongue." The words we speak do make a difference. James says, "The tongue is a small member of our body, yet it boasts of great exploits."

There's the old colloquialism: "Sticks and stones may break my bones, but words will never hurt me." Not true. Words have started wars, but they have also brought about peace. Words have torn apart relationships, but they have also restored them.

James said, "Out of the abundance of the heart, the mouth speaks." I interpret that to mean what we say is who we are. We are defined by what it is we communicate to other people. Do we build up and encourage and uplift, or do we tear down and break apart and destroy?

It's interesting to note that when we think about what it is we say to other people in the world in which we live today, the lasting effect can either encourage or diminish. But it's always been that way. We just have more means of being able to do it than ever before in our history.

Now, think about it for a moment. The words that you speak and the words that you hear are significant, because in a variety of ways they shape us. The words we speak define who we are, establish our reputation. The words that we hear oftentimes determine our self-image, our self-worth, our self-esteem.

So, what we should realize is that when we speak, whatever it is we say and to whomever it is we say it, we must remember we're either encouraging and uplifting and giving life, or we are breaking down, tearing apart, and taking a life away from someone else. Either the light of Jesus Christ speaks for us, or the darkness of evil has a word from our mouth.

The book of Proverbs says, "A soothing tongue is the tree of life. A perverse tongue crushes the spirit." James says in his New Testament book, "The tongue is a fire." If it is a fire, then do we use our tongue to refine or use our tongue to consume? What we say determines who we are and oftentimes shapes the relationships we have with other people—either in a positive way or with an eternal lasting and negative effect on others. There is extraordinary power in the words that we speak one way or another.

But because we live in the twenty-first century, we have means of communication that go well beyond just what it is we say. We know that we can send nasty emails or we can post something on Facebook that puts down someone else or belittles or causes us to whine and complain. We can find all kinds of ways to communicate who we are to other people and what it is we think about any given topic.

And there are, as we know, lots of people who choose to send negative information out to the world as if everybody is waiting with bated breath to hear what it is they think about any given topic or individual. But it is not our role as followers of Jesus Christ to try to find something wrong with someone else and then let the rest of the world know it.

James had an interesting dilemma. He was the half-brother of Jesus. And James found himself in the position in the early days of the church of witnessing to Christians who said and professed one thing, and oftentimes their lifestyles contradicted the very thing they stated they believed.

So, James wanted to make it abundantly clear we should be very intentional about every word that we speak—whatever it is we say, and to whomever it is we say it—because it makes a lasting imprint. It has an eternal effect on other people, either positively or negatively. It's up to us. There is great power in the tongue, and it's our role in the world to try to tame the tongue, as James spoke—that is, to use it in the right way, not to destroy, but to build up and encourage.

For many years in my ministry, I had a man in a great position of authority over me. Every time I was around him, for whatever reason, he constantly put me down. Now, most of the time he tried to couch it in humor. He would say things like, "Clearly, you got your hair cut by a blind barber!"

Couching put-downs with humor is in some ways even more insidious and evil than just saying it, because you're being manipulative and you always have an out. "Oh, I was just kidding. Why are you offended?"

That man did that to me over and again, and I thought, *What did I do to offend him that he would say something like that to me every single time I was around him?* But later, I noticed he did it with everybody. I wasn't unique. That's the way he communicated. So I finally decided that the best thing I could do, when I saw him come into the room, was either go to the other side of the room or exit the room altogether. I just wasn't going to tolerate it. It wasn't good for me, and his manner was destructive. It caused me to be very self-conscious, and I didn't need that.

73

And sometimes, I have wondered in my own life, have I ever entered a room and someone else walked out because I came in? Have I ever couched put-downs with humor or ever just belittled someone else, and it hurt so much they literally did not want to be in my presence? I pray to God that I haven't, but I'm not sure that's true.

We ought to be the kind of people in the world in which we live today where put-downs and destructive communication cannot be a part of the makeup of who we are. Enough people are doing it in the world as it is. We need to be contrary to the world sometimes, and as followers of Jesus Christ, it is our role to speak life into other people, not to take life from them.

If you look at Jesus, our Lord had many opportunities to speak to many, many people, and oftentimes He would speak in such a way that those who had felt excluded before suddenly felt included. They were somebody, they mattered because Jesus said so. Jesus spoke words of comfort. "Blessed are those who mourn, for they shall be comforted."

He spoke words of encouragement to people who were considered dirty and unclean. When he said to them, "It's your faith that made you well," it's an affirmation that because their belief was so strong they took care of their own condition.

When Jesus recognized the downtrodden and those previously ignored, declaring to them: "You're a daughter of Abraham" and "You're a son of Abraham," that meant that, "The world may have said you're a nobody and you're an outcast and you belong over there; but I'm telling you, you're a part of the family. You matter." Can you imagine what it must be like to be isolated and alienated from people because you've been made to feel unworthy, only to be told by God in flesh that you matter to God forever?

Jesus Christ found many ways to include people, to build them up, to encourage them. He even gave instruction. "Do this in remembrance of me. Take this bread and take this cup. Take me into yourself. I want to be so close to you that I am a part of you." Now, can you imagine that kind of love being expressed to you and that kind of love being expressed to me? It's extraordinary to think about.

Jesus found so many occasions to say something that gave life to other people. And if we emulate the life of Jesus and live like he did, then it's our role and our responsibility to do the same. We can all be critical of other people. People can always be critical of us. We can always find fault with someone else, and they can always find fault with us. That's easy. That doesn't take any talent. Anybody can do that.

But what takes faith and a determined approach to life is to look at the good qualities in human beings and expose that to the world. Because I promise you, the more you say that's good to someone else, the better they become in so many ways. But the opposite is also true. The more negative you are to them, the more spiteful they become. It's just true for all of us.

Our responsibility is to tame the tongue. In the same way you put a bit and bridle in the mouth of a horse to direct it where you want it to go, or you have a rudder to direct your ship or your boat wherever you want it to go, the tongue can make a difference where we send other people. We either send them into darkness and despair or we send them to a place of light and life. And it can all depend on how we use, as James says, that small member of our body that boasts of great exploits. To build on James's passage is a verse from Proverbs chapter 12 which informs us that, "Words of the reckless pierce like a sword, but the tongue of the wise brings healing."

I think sometimes the people we are closest to, the people we are around most often, are oftentimes the ones who get the most criticism. We criticize our respective spouse over and again, or our children, or coworkers, or pastors, or others near us because they're easy prey.

And some of us have become accustomed to doing that to such a degree that we live a dysfunctional life and don't even realize it. And what we or others do is spend an inordinate amount of time trying to find something wrong with someone else, and we don't even know it.

We must be very intentional about how it is that we speak to other people in the world today where there's so much vitriol, so much hatred, so much anger. There are people who are always seemingly looking for a reason to put others down.

Years ago, I had a good, close friend. He was a great guy, kind of a young Renaissance man, who taught himself how to play several instruments. He was athletic, good-looking, had a great sense of humor, fun to be around, and a dear friend of mine.

But for whatever reason, and to this day I really don't know why, his parents didn't feel the same way about him, probably because they had a problem with alcohol. They were always putting him down and belittling him in front of me and other people. It was humiliating for him, but they did it time and time again. He never seemed to measure up for them. He was never good enough. He was always going to be compared to someone else, and he would always fall short over and again.

I remember one day being at his house, after his father had lifted his elbow one too many times to the Scotch bottle. He came up to me and said, "John, let me see your fingernails." I said, "I beg your pardon?" He said, "Let me see your fingernails." I said, "Okay." Then he called his son over and demanded, "Let me see your fingernails."

"Dad, please!"

"*Son*, show me your fingernails."

He stuck out his hands toward his dad.

And father said to son, "Why can't you have well-manicured and clean fingernails like John? Why do your fingernails have to look the way they do?"

And in that moment, I thought to myself, "Dear God in heaven, he has put his son down so many times, he's run out of excuses to belittle him. So now he's looking at the fingernails of other people just to denigrate him again."

There are people like that in the world. They're all over the place, and they love to post things. They love to say things. They love to make it obvious. Why are they like that? What creates the level of insecurity within them to cause them to feel like the only way they can build themselves up is to embarrass, to belittle, to put down others.

You see, in the life of the church, it's our role to live in such a way that we are encouraging, and we are uplifting like Jesus Christ. To also show that we are inclusive, that we find a way to express love and say it over and again. And for people to feel safe and secure and loved.

Plus, it's our responsibility to be as careful as we can about taming the tongue.

James said of the tongue, it can be "a restless evil, full of deadly poison … Out of the same mouth, come praise and cursing. It ought not to be so."

There's a story about a teenage boy who was always negative and always saying something destructive to someone else, and his father had had enough of it. He called the boy in and said, "Son, I want you to be aware of how often you're critical toward other people and the negative things you say. So, every time I hear you say something negative, you take a nail, I want you to go out to the back fence, and I want you to nail that nail into the wooden fence."

Time and again, his father would have him go out to the fence and put yet another nail in it. Eventually the back fence had nails all over its surface. The father called his son over one day and said, "I want you to look at this. Look at all the nails of all the negative things you've said about other people. Enough is enough. I want you to be intentional now about saying something good and positive and encouraging to other people. And every time you do that, I'm going to have you come out and pull one of the nails out of the fence."

The young man became very intentional and very careful about saying good and positive comments to other people. And he came to find great joy in being able to go out and pull one nail after another from the fence until, finally, one day all the nails were gone.

His dad called him back over to the fence and said, "I want to tell you how proud I am of you. This used to be filled with nails, and now all of the nails are gone because you've said so many kind things to other people." Kind of smugly, the young boy said, "See, Dad, I did it. I did what you told me to do." Then the father said, "But I want you to look at the fence. Notice that the fence is scarred from now on. No matter what you have said, what you said originally has caused this fence to be scarred, and those scars remain."

We always want to say, "I'm sorry." We always want to say, "I wish I hadn't said it. I apologize." But we said it. Then we apologized and tried to take it back. But sometimes the scars are still there, even though we apologized and atoned. Kind of like that person who said, "Yes, I forgave, but I'll never forget." But maybe what's more important is that we think about what it is that we say *before* we say it, and when we think about it, something encouraging and uplifting and Christ-like comes out of our mouth instead of some way to put down or belittle. That way, you also don't leave any scars.

You have every chance in the world to belittle, and you have every chance in the world to uplift and encourage. It's on you to make a difference. We either speak for Jesus Christ or we speak for the devil. We either bring light into the life of someone else or we cast a darkness over who they are. We either give them life or we take life from them. The choice is ours.

May we do our best to remember it's our role to tame the tongue, to speak like Jesus, to encourage and promote love, saying kind words, uplifting words—words that give life, beautiful words, wonderful words, wonderful words of life.

Hallelujah. Amen.

Set Apart from the Start

> *Now the word of the Lord came to me saying, "Before I formed you in the womb I knew you, and before you were born I consecrated you; I appointed you a prophet to the nations." Then I said, "Ah, Lord God! Truly I do not know how to speak, for I am only a boy." But the Lord said to me, "Do not say, 'I am only a boy,' for you shall go to all to whom I send you, and you shall speak whatever I command you. Do not be afraid of them, for I am with you to deliver you, says the Lord." Then the Lord put out his hand and touched my mouth, and the Lord said to me, "Now I have put my words in your mouth. See, today I appoint you over nations and over kingdoms, to pluck up and to pull down, to destroy and to overthrow, to build and to plant."*
>
> —JEREMIAH 1:4–10

I have two brothers who are also ordained pastors. One is older than I am, and one is younger. We grew up in the same house. We had the same set of parents. We grew up with the same teachings. We went to church on Sunday morning, went to the same schools. We did things that a family would do together. We grew up, really, in a lot of ways, as one. But my two brothers and I, though we have all three been called to the ordained ministry, are very different from one another.

My older brother, Tom, is cerebral, but he lives on a ranch in addition to successfully pastoring his substantial church and all that goes with it. He also has cattle and horses, and he loves to ride his tractor and repair broken fences and weld; he just loves being outdoors, period.

My younger brother, Joel, was in the U.S. Army and the Marine Corps, and he's rough as a cob. He is also a United Methodist pastor, and he loves to shoot his guns and hunt and fish and ride his motorcycle.

And then there's me. I like to put on a coat and tie and visit museums and attend the symphony. We three are very, very different. But all of us have been called by God to a specific task and a certain responsibility.

But that's the case with all of God's children. We're all different. Every one of us is unique. There has never been nor will there ever be anyone just like us.

And like my two brothers and me, every one of us has been called by God, set apart from our beginning to be who it is God would have us to be, and to reach the potential that God put in place for every single one of us. Like the prophet Jeremiah, we have been set apart from the start.

One day God called Jeremiah with a specific task and a certain responsibility. God said, "I formed you in the womb. Before you were born, I set you apart. I appointed you as a prophet." God knew and God appointed, and God set apart Jeremiah for a specific task, a certain responsibility. But God does that for all of us. God sets a certain task and a specific responsibility for every single one of us. We are born into the world with a purpose, a reason for being. And God has given us the skill set and the talent to achieve whatever it is God has called us to do, all we are to do for the kingdom of God.

But notice the response of Jeremiah. Jeremiah did not want that responsibility. He said, "I don't speak well." Sounded a lot like what Moses said when God called him. Remember that? And then he said, "I'm too young. I don't speak well. I'm too young. God, how can you set me apart to be a prophet to the nations when I'm so inexperienced, so young, and I don't speak well? I'm not a good public speaker." And God said, in essence to Jeremiah, "Do not fear. I'm going to give you everything you need to do what I've set apart for you to do."

If you notice in scripture, there were several occasions when God called people who were extremely young to do things well beyond their years. Think about it for a moment. David was the youngest of all his brothers. The most insignificant, if you will, at least in the eyes of that culture and that day and time, because of his young age. And yet, Samuel called him out and anointed him to be the king of Israel. Scripture tells us that David was so young he had ruddy cheeks (those red cheeks that little boys have). That's who he was. And yet, even in his young age, he was called out by God. Because God knew, God set him apart to do what it was God would have him do.

And we certainly know about Mary. She was a young teenage virgin and given the most extraordinary of responsibilities, chosen to give birth to and raise the Savior of the world—God in flesh. She had no experience with a man and virtually no experience living life. And yet, God set her apart for that specific task, because God gave her the skill set necessary to do what God needed her to do, even if she didn't know it.

And then there is the apostle Paul, who was not young himself, but one of his protégés was. Timothy was very young, but Paul relied very heavily on him to get the gospel message out to support Paul's ministry. And notably, Paul wrote to Timothy and told him, "Don't let people look down on you because you are young."

Jeremiah's excuse of being so young was not going to work with God. God said, "I set you apart from the very start to do what I need you to do."

John the Baptist was set apart from the start with the responsibility of one day preparing everyone for the presence of the anointed one, Jesus Christ himself. John was born set apart for that specific task. And then there is, of course, Jesus himself, set apart from the start to do what God would have Christ do in the world, and that is save the world.

And then there is you … and there is me. We are a people, individually and collectively, who have been called by God. Don't believe for a moment that you haven't been called by God. It may not be to the ordained ministry. It may not be to be prophetic. But it is indeed a calling from God to do good for the kingdom. Everybody born into the world has been given a task and a skill set to do what God would have you to do, to reach your potential as God has established for you.

I love what Frederick Buechner said in his book *Wishful Thinking*. He wrote, "The place God calls you is the place where your deep gladness and the world's deep hunger meet." In other words, God created you with the capacity to do something good, to place you in a position and among people to do what you can do fully and completely with what it is God has given you to achieve whatever it is God would have you accomplish.

There is no one like you. That's extraordinary to think about. Of the billions and billions of people on Planet Earth now and the billions who have gone before us and will come after us, not one other person is just like you. No one has your exact skill set, your intellect, your charm, your wit, your sense of humor, your capacity to do good, your sensitivity. Nobody has it just like you have it, which means God took a lot of time and a lot of thought in creating you and bringing you into this world. You, like Jeremiah, have been set apart from the start.

No one is born into the world purposeless. No one is born into existence without meaning. Everybody has a purpose, everybody has potential, and everybody has meaning and a reason for being here. Our task is to try to determine what that is; to be sensitive to how it is that God comes to us and people and events and circumstances in life; to be sensitive to the way God presents us in a certain moment with a certain skill set. That requires prayer, it requires worship, it requires scripture reading, it requires thinking that every day God has something in store for you that is good to do.

Every one of us has been called and set apart from the very beginning to be people of love and forgiveness and mercy and grace. God doesn't create anyone ever to do anything but good. Now, we oftentimes choose to do that which is contrary to who it is God would have us to be, but that's on us.

The truth is you have something that God has called you to do, and you are supposed to be the person God has called you to be. You have everything at your disposal to make that happen in every way.

Your real vocation is as a Christian. Now, you may be already employed, and you might be a professional in some way, but your primary vocation is being a Christian. That is, Christ is first, always in your life, and he should always determine how you live out the rest of your life on any level, whatever it may be. We seek first the kingdom of God, says scripture, and his righteousness, and all things will be given to us as a result.

There are people who act as though they were born into the world with no real purpose or meaning. They could care less about other people. They don't ever make an effort to step in and help. They're not going to forgive. They're not going to extend grace. They're certainly not going to show mercy. There are people like that, but that is of their own choosing. They weren't born into the world to be that way. They've chosen to be that way. Every one of us was born in the world to do good. So what is your calling? Who are you supposed to be?

What is it about who you are that makes such a profound difference for the sake of the kingdom of God in the world? You have been set apart from the start to figure out who you are and what you're supposed to do. Every one of us has some level of talent and skill, although I've said it many times, and I've heard other people say it many times, "I just don't have any kind of talent." Because oftentimes we compare our skill set with the skill set of other people.

I'm not artistic. I can't sing. I'm not a musician. I don't have any of those skills. I don't have that talent. I don't think abstractly. Everything is concrete for me. I must work hard to understand any kind of poetry or what a painting is supposed to represent. I want to, because I like to go to museums, but oftentimes I have to have someone explain to me what that's all about. I wasn't born with some of the skills I want. But that's okay. You weren't born with all the skills that you want, either. Your responsibility is to figure out how to exploit the strengths God has given you for the greater good and for the glory of God.

God never calls anybody—now listen to this—into the world to be manipulative or conniving or to create harm. No one has been born into the world to do that, but people do it all the time. That means we have turned our back on the very person God has called us to be when we do those kinds of things. But we were set apart from the start just like Jeremiah, to be who it is God would have us to be fully and completely. And sometimes in the process of being that way, it is confusing for others. Because you will notice, as I mentioned earlier, Jeremiah was very young.

But God has called people in scripture and God has called people to this very day who are not always young to do what it is God would have them to do. We know when the floods came, Noah had built an ark. But did you know when those floods arrived, Noah was six hundred years old? Now, I'm telling you, if I lived six hundred years and God said go build an ark, I'd say, "Lord, time out. I really am too old for that. I mean, I can't build an ark. That's another skill I don't have."

Our responsibility is to do what we have been called to do. If it is good and it is for the kingdom, then it is of God. Regardless of age, young or old or somewhere in the middle

... and even if other people see it is irresponsible, if it is for good, it must be from God.

Let me give you an example of what I mean. My daddy graduated from The Citadel in Charleston, South Carolina, was commissioned into the United States Army, went to Tulane Law School and graduated with his law degree, and then entered the JAG Corps. And while he was in the army, he was a judge. He was a military judge, and he was sent to Vietnam. He was in Vietnam for a year. Then he came home, got out of the army, and practiced law in the civilian world for a period of time.

But my father always wrestled with a call to ministry. He had four children at home (small young children at the time), and he was making really good money in his law practice. And one day he decided that was enough. And my father told his partners he was leaving his law practice. He had decided that he was going to go back to school, to seminary. He would end up in a small town with a small church with a much smaller level of income than he had had previously.

And my father caught all kinds of grief from other family members, and certainly from those with whom he had been working. They said, "You're irresponsible to do this to your family. You're not thinking straight. God wouldn't be asking you to do this." But my father pushed on and had a remarkable career as a United Methodist pastor—a highly, highly successful ministry.

But he wasn't twenty-two when he was called. He was much older than that. And sometimes when we are called to be who God would have us to be and do what it is God would have us to do—at whatever age, whatever level of income, where we are, and what our status may be in life—some people may be critical, may not understand.

But if God calls us, it must be for the greater good—for the greater good of humanity, for the greater good of the kingdom. God doesn't call people to harm or to hurt. God calls us instead to plant and to build up and to do great good. When Moses and his brother Aaron had to finally confront Pharaoh, having been led by God, Moses was eighty and Aaron was eighty-three. And they did it because they'd been called to do it.

Think about people in your own life who are older, who might believe that somehow they've reached a point in life where they've done all that they can do—that there's nothing left, no other opportunity, nothing available to them to make a difference.

But that's simply not true, because we've all been set apart from the start, and whatever skill set we have, whatever capacity we have to do great good, stays with us in some way or other. And it is our role and our responsibility to live it out to the very end. God still calls people of all ages every day to do things both large and small, but all of it can be so incredibly impactful, if we will be who it is God calls us to be, the way God has called us to live.

Gideon was called by God to lead an army against the Midianites. Scripture tells us that Gideon was the youngest in his family. And God said to Gideon, "I need you to do this," and Gideon repeatedly said, "I don't want it. I don't want to do it. Prove to me this is God speaking to me. And, by the way, God, why would we be in this mess if you're with us like you say? Why wouldn't you be with us? Why are we in such a mess?" I mean, Gideon went toe to toe with God! But guess who won? Guess who always wins! And Gideon did what God called him to do, and he did it successfully even in his young age.

Set apart from the start, you have the skills, you have the knowledge, you have the know-how, you have the experience, you have the wisdom. It's on you. God has gifted you. How are you going to do whatever it is you will do for the greater good of the kingdom?

You have what you need to be who God has called you to be, to reach your full potential. It is within you. By the power of the Holy Spirit may you live it out, and may I live out my calling as well, as best we can. And if we all did it, oh what a world this could be.

Hallelujah. Amen.

What *Forgiveness* Does

> Have mercy on me, O God, according to your steadfast love; according to your abundant mercy, blot out my transgressions. Wash me thoroughly from my iniquity and cleanse me from my sin. For I know my transgressions, and my sin is ever before me. Against you, you alone, have I sinned and done what is evil in your sight, so that you are justified in your sentence and blameless when you pass judgment. Indeed, I was born guilty, a sinner when my mother conceived me. You desire truth in the inward being; therefore teach me wisdom in my secret heart. Purge me with hyssop, and I shall be clean; wash me, and I shall be whiter than snow. Let me hear joy and gladness; let the bones that you have crushed rejoice. Hide your face from my sins and blot out all my iniquities. Create in me a clean heart, O God, and put a new and right spirit within me. Do not cast me away from your presence, and do not take your holy spirit from me. Restore to me the joy of your salvation, and sustain in me a willing spirit.
>
> —PSALM 51:1–12

A number of years ago, early in my ministry, I was serving a church that had absolutely no staff other than me. I was the youth director and the custodian. I was in charge of the United Methodist Women's Group, and I mowed the lawns. Plus, I cleaned the bathrooms and did every other job of any kind that the church needed doing. I did it all. Finally, the church raised enough money to have a part-time secretary.

But it was a little bitty facility, which meant she had to also share the church office with me. The office was simply converted from one of the small Sunday school rooms, which, when reconfigured to house us both to work at our desks, put her in a position where her back faced me. She was up there just a few hours a week to put together the bulletin for Sunday mornings and the monthly newsletter. But when we were in conversation, I was always looking at her back.

One day, she came into the office wearing a beautiful new silk blouse. She looked very pretty. She sat down. In fact, I commented on her beautiful apparel. As is my custom, I began my work at my desk. And when I write, I write with a fountain pen. I have for years. I write my sermons with a fountain pen and do all my correspondence with one. I love writing with a fountain pen. But there is a problem on occasion with one such writing instrument, and that is they will clog. And when that happens, the easiest way to unclog them is to shake them up and down. It loosens up the ink in the barrel.

My part-time secretary, with her back to me, was sitting there one morning when I suddenly found myself with a clogged pen. I began to shake that pen with a few pretty firm shakes to loosen up the ink and successfully continued to write. A bit later, I looked up and discovered that I had hosed down the back of that beautiful blouse with fountain pen ink. I mean, I had doused that thing. I had unleashed a fury of ink all over her back, and she hadn't yet noticed. And for a moment, I thought, *I'm not going to tell her.*

But I knew I couldn't do that. I knew that in any moment she was going to wonder what in the world happened, especially when her back began to sense that it was wet. And I said, "Please turn around and look at me. I am mortified at what I have done. I have hosed down your back with ink." She said, "Haha, real funny." But I responded, "I promise you, I am not making it up." So, she got up and went into the bathroom and came back in a few minutes later and said, "Yes, you did. You hosed down my blouse."

In an attempt to apologize, I said, "Listen, I promise you, let's go right now to the store, and I'll buy you a new one. Plus, you can have the rest of the day off. Take the rest of the month off as far as I'm concerned. I can't believe I would do something so stupid." But after an uncomfortable few moments of silence, she finally said, "Do you mind if I go home and change?" I answered, "Of course not. And stay home, please, if you'd like." She said, "I'm going to go home to change, and I'll come back."

She came back in a little while, sat down. and continued her work. I begged her to forgive me. Over and again, I said, "I am so sorry that I did this. I cannot believe I did it." And finally, she turned around, looked at me, and said, "Stop. You did it. You said you were sorry. Now let's move on."

I think that's exactly what God says to us at times. When we mess up, when we make a mistake and come before God, we say, "God, please forgive me. I am sorry for what I have done." And God says, "You know what? That's enough. You did it. You said you were sorry. Now let's move on."

A long time ago, there was a man by the name of David who ascended to the throne, the king of Israel, a man of great power and influence. And one day as he looks out a window, he sees a beautiful woman bathing, and he has to have her as his own. The problem is she's already married, but that doesn't stop David at all. He takes her as his own.

She then conceives a child from David. And David ponders what to do next, because she's married to somebody else. He hatches a plan. When Uriah, Bathsheba's husband, comes home, David tries to persuade him to spend time with his wife. Uriah comes in from the battlefield, and David calls him in and tells him, "You go home. You have worked hard. Enjoy time with your wife." To David's shock and surprise, Uriah says, "I will not. I need to save all my energy and all my efforts to be a part of the army."

David doesn't know what to do, so he hatches another plan. This time he gives instructions that Uriah is to be sent to the front lines of the battle. And then the rest of the troops are to leave him there, vulnerable, which they do— and Uriah dies in battle.

David thinks he's off the hook. Now he can take Bathsheba as his wife, with no one being the wiser. But David has committed adultery and has multiplied his debauchery by hatching a plan for one of his most faithful and loyal soldiers to be put to death.

But to further complicate matters, there is another problem. Soon afterward, the prophet Nathan approaches David and declares, "I know what you have done, and more importantly, God knows what you have done. You are a sinful man." Under enormous guilt, David breaks down and recognizes his sin. With remorse, David pens what we call

Psalm 51, which is his way of coming before God and say-ing, "Cleanse me, wash me, purge me, make me whiter than snow." David is pouring himself out before God, asking to be forgiven. And as heinous as his acts were, we believe in a God who says, "You did it, you said you were sorry, now let's move on."

That's the unique gift of forgiveness. We believe in a God who is ready, willing, and able to give us another shot, another chance, and is willing to enable us to move beyond our past failures into a new and brighter day.

In 1 John, John writes, "If we confess our sin, he who is faithful and just will forgive our sin and cleanse us from all unrighteousness." It doesn't matter what we have done. God's love and capacity to forgive are greater than any sin we could commit. But we must be sincerely sorry, and we must repent. We have to have that level of regret that acknowledges we have done wrong, and we need that for-giveness.

The most common word in the New Testament for for-giveness in the Greek means to fling, hurl, release, and to let go of whatever it is that has shackled us, whatever it is that causes us pain because of our unwillingness to forgive someone who may have harmed us or someone we love.

The extraordinary thing about forgiveness is that it is a gift given to us by God, a gift that we can receive—but it is also a gift that we can give away. It is a gift we can give to ourselves when we finally reach a point of being able to for-give, and when we're no longer shackled by the resentment and the anger.

Forgiveness is a gift we can give someone else. It nev-er means condoning or acknowledging that somehow now what they did is okay. It can still be wrong. It can still hurt. But forgiveness enables us to leave the past and move into the future with hope and appreciate the present, not burdened by our anger or our resentment or our guilt or our shame or whatever it may be—to hurl it, to fling it, to release it. That's what God does for us.

The thing about forgiveness is, as someone once said, when we genuinely forgive, we set a prisoner free and then we discover that that prisoner is us. Forgiveness shackles us. It chains us to the past.

But it is not easy. I'm a human being like everybody else, and I know how hard that is. But I hope and pray that every time I have ever gone before God and asked to be forgiven for something—something I have done that I wish I hadn't, or something I have left undone that I should have done—that there is a God greater than anything I may have done who has the capacity to forgive me.

But that same God expects us to do it in return. Resentment means literally to feel all over again. And who wants to feel that pain all over again? Forgiveness allows us to move beyond that.

In 2012, Craig Erickson, age seventy-three, was sentenced to life in prison for murder; he had killed his high school classmate at the age of seventy-two. It seems that for a lifetime, Craig Erickson held bitterness and anger toward his classmate who, more than fifty years earlier, had committed some kind of locker room prank on Erickson. And for all those years he let that anger seethe and grow, let that bitterness become all-consuming to the point that, at the age of seventy-two he knocked on the door of Norman

Johnson's house, and when he opened the door, Craig Erickson shot him dead.

Those fifty-plus years of growing bitterness and anger had destroyed him. If only he'd learned to let go, to hurl, to fling, to accept the gift of forgiveness and to also give that gift to someone else.

Listen, we all recognize forgiveness is not easy, but one of the things we need to do is take scripture seriously and follow Jesus Christ and his teachings that we must learn to forgive.

Jesus said to Peter, "You don't forgive seven times." You can imagine in the moment that Peter is grateful. Who in the world wants to forgive somebody as many as seven times? And then Jesus adds a caveat, "Not seven times, but seventy times seven." An infinite number of times you have a responsibility to forgive. Jesus made that mandate clear. And then he turned around and taught his disciples the Lord's Prayer, and we say, "Forgive us our trespasses, as we forgive those who trespass against us." And then Jesus proved it himself by hanging on the cross and writhing in unimaginable pain, saying, "Father, forgive them, for they know not what they do."

There is the expectation that we are a people of forgiveness, and it's not easy. We all know that. But if we can accept the gift from God, it is our responsibility, says scripture, that we turn around and give that gift away. If we are unwilling to forgive, scripture is clear: we don't receive forgiveness. And that means the effort of Jesus Christ on the cross was a futile effort on our behalf if we're not willing to forgive.

In all my years of ministry, this is the single greatest problem I think I have seen when couples come into my office with marital issues. It's not money issues. It's not infidelity. It's their unwillingness to let go, unwillingness to forgive each other for even the pettiest of things. And it just builds up and gets stronger and greater, and their resentment grows over time.

Unforgiveness is a cancer in the life of every human being. And there is a gift that can free us from all that pain and sorrow and resentment and regret and shame in whatever form it may present itself. It's our responsibility to accept it.

Now, here's what I find interesting. If you will notice, David does not ask to be forgiven until he's been caught. In fact, he thought he got away with it. It is only after he is caught that he recognizes his grievous mistakes, his deep sin, but he asks God, and God forgives him. Remember the story of the prodigal son. He rushes home to be back with his father only after he has run out of food and money. But the father still embraces him.

And there are instances in our life when the only time we really ask to be forgiven is when we finally reach a point where we have exhausted every other means of justifying or rationalizing what we have done.

And sometimes, out of sheer desperation, we come before God, and the good news is—like David, like the prodigal son—when we've come before God only when we have been exposed, God still says, "You did it. You said you were sorry. Now let's move on." All because of what Jesus Christ did for us on the cross, taking upon himself all the sin of all of humanity for all of time and dying to that sin, an extraordinary gift, but a gift we must accept and a gift we need to share in return.

I have lived my share of years, and I can tell you this—There have been many occasions in my life when I have begged someone to forgive me. And there have been many times in life when I have had to forgive someone or struggled with forgiveness. And you know what that is like as well. You live in this world. You have been there. Forgiveness is not always easy. And there are occasions in life when things happen that are so awful we wonder whether anybody would ever have the capacity to forgive what has been done.

If you will notice in scripture, there is no timetable on forgiveness. Jesus never says when you have been hurt, you need to forgive within the first hour. Or you've got to do it by the end of the day, even by the end of the week. But there is an expectation that we do forgive, and some things take longer, and some struggles are harder than others. And I do think that God appreciates our effort to try to reach a point to forgive even if we are not there yet.

Years ago, I read a book by Philip Yancey called *What's So Amazing About Grace*, which is a masterpiece. I would recommend it to anybody. In it, Philip Yancey tells a story about Larry Trapp. Larry Trapp was a grand dragon in the KKK, a high-ranking official in the Ku Klux Klan, a man filled with vitriol and anger, a bigot, a racist who used his influence and power to try to destroy. There was one Jewish family that oftentimes was the target of Larry Trapp's anger. He'd frequently try to do something to cause that family harm or pain.

As time went by, Larry Trapp got sicker and sicker with severe diabetes, among other major health issues that caused him to be in a position where he was dependent on others to care for him. But for whatever reason, his fellow KKK members didn't or wouldn't pitch in. But guess who took him into their home? It was that same Jewish family to whom he had tried to cause so much harm for so many years. They brought him into their home. They forgave him. They loved him. They showed him compassion.

Larry Trapp would eventually renounce anything that had to do with his past. He gave in and started the process of trying to ask to be forgiven. He gave up all the literature that he produced and the Nazi flags that hung in his home. Everything that he had done that somehow indicated his past he tried to toss and disown. And all because a Jewish family who he tried to harm forgave him and began the process of loving him and caring for him in his greatest time of need. Forgiveness is a gift. Forgiveness is life-giving.

And we believe in a God we know in and through Jesus Christ, no matter what we have done, no matter what we have left undone, who says, "I forgive you." You've got another shot at it. But we sincerely have to repent. We must be genuine about our remorse. And then we move on. Remember, God says to all of us, and we need to say to each other, "You did it. You said you were sorry. Now let's move on."

Hallelujah. Amen.

As a Disciple
of Jesus

The Greatest *of These...*

If I speak in the tongues of humans and of angels but do not have love, I am a noisy gong or a clanging cymbal. And if I have prophetic powers and understand all mysteries and all knowledge and if I have all faith so as to remove mountains but do not have love, I am nothing. If I give away all my possessions and if I hand over my body so that I may boast but do not have love, I gain nothing. Love is patient; love is kind; love is not envious or boastful or arrogant or rude. It does not insist on its own way; it is not irritable; it keeps no record of wrongs; it does not rejoice in wrongdoing but rejoices in the truth. It bears all things, believes all things, hopes all things, endures all things. Love never ends. But as for prophecies, they will come to an end; as for tongues, they will cease; as for knowledge, it will come to an end. For we know only in part, and we prophesy only in part, but when the complete comes, the partial will come to an end. When I was a child, I spoke like a child, I thought like a child, I reasoned like a child. When I became an adult, I put an end to childish ways. For now we see only a reflection, as in a mirror, but then we will see face to face. Now I know only in part; then I will know fully, even as I have been fully known. And now faith, hope, and love remain; these three, and the greatest of these is love.

—1 CORINTHIANS 13:1–13

*W*e all know those three words that we can never say enough or hear enough, regardless of our age or our gender: "I LOVE YOU." I love to say it. I love to hear it. And that's the case with you as well. There are people, of course, who are so desperate to be loved that they'll even compromise their morals. They'll allow themselves to be taken advantage of in search of love. And the reason we have such a desperate need to say that we are loved, to hear that we are loved, and to speak those words of love, is because we are created in the image of love. It is an inherent part of the makeup of who we are.

"God is love," we read in 1 John—the simple definition of who God is, which means if we're created in the image of God, we are created in the image of love. We need it like we need food and drink. In fact, Jesus said the two greatest commandments are to love God and love our neighbor. We are commanded to love. It is an inherent part of the make-up of who we are. It is a desire. It is a need. It is a want that every one of us without exception long for.

You've never heard anybody say, "I am so sick and tired of people telling me they love me." I can't imagine hearing that. It is never enough. It's like having a meal. And then a few hours later, you're ready for another one. Hearing "I love you" is something we appreciate and want, but then we need to hear it again.

Spouses need to say it to each other every day. Parents need to say it to their children, and children need to say it to their parents. Friends need to say it to each other and hear it from one another. And God is the one who says in so many ways to us every single day, "I love you". And it is our responsibility to say back to God, "I love you, too." God wants to hear it as much as we do.

I've said before, I have a fascination with Fred Rogers, Mr. Rogers. I loved that man as a little boy, and I still love him even though he's been dead for more than twenty years. His legacy is extraordinary. And one of the things that I always appreciated about Fred Rogers himself was that he weighed 143 pounds and was obsessed with that.

He didn't want to weigh 142. He didn't want to weigh 144. He didn't want to weigh anything other than 143 pounds. And every day he weighed himself to make sure that he maintained that weight. You know why? Because the numbers 143 were so representative of his life, and he saw that as a mandate.

I: one letter. LOVE: four letters. YOU: three letters = 143.

So, Fred Rogers always wanted to weigh 143 pounds, so he was literally the visible presence of love.

Now, that's extraordinary, right? Now look, some of us are never going to weigh 143 pounds again. And that's okay. But like Fred Rogers, we can be the personification of love. We can share it. We can show it. It doesn't matter how much money we have. It doesn't matter what kind of influence we have. It doesn't matter where we live or our level of education. All those kinds of things are extraordinary achievements and accomplishments, but the greatest achievement is to be loved. That's the one thing all of us want no matter what our age or gender may be.

So the apostle Paul wrote to the church in Corinth what we know to be the love chapter.

"Love is not envious or boastful," he says. "It is not arrogant or rude. It does not insist on its own way. Love never ends." But we all know that love takes lots of work because we can get irritated with each other. We can get frustrated. We can even get mad at one another. But the overriding, overarching theme of our relationship with anybody we care about should be love.

I remember years ago, I had a mother call me one day and say, "Can my third-grade daughter come meet with you?" I didn't know the little girl, and I really didn't know the parents well, but the mom and dad were getting a divorce, and they shared the news with their only child, their third-grade daughter. They wanted me to be able to visit with her as her pastor and talk through that. I said, "Well, sure. You can bring her up to the church."

So she came into my office. Mommy waited outside, and the little third-grade girl said, "Mommy and Daddy told me they can't keep their promises they made to one another and they made to God anymore. They said they can't keep their vows. Now, what are vows?" And I said, "Vows are promises."

And she said, as innocently and as sincerely as she could, "Does that mean that my mommy and daddy, because they're getting a divorce, have to stand in front of God and say their vows backwards?" Wow! See, love is such an inherent part of the makeup of who we are.

Notice what Paul said. "When I was a child, I spoke like a child. I thought like a child. I reasoned like a child. But when I became an adult, I put an end to childish ways." What Paul means is, I became a little more spiritually mature, and I realized how important love is. But children know that too. They're born with that desire, that need.

I know there are people who will say, "Listen, I'm just not good at saying 'I love you.'" You know, those are usually the same people who can say three other words together really well, like, "Where's my beer? Rub my feet? Scratch my back?" But they can't say, "I love you"? Come on! It's a part of the makeup of who people are. Everybody can say it. Everybody can show it. And everybody needs it.

Certainly, in the life of the church, we have an obligation and responsibility to do that. I've heard people say many times, "I don't need to tell my spouse I love them; I married them, didn't I?" And they usually say it just like that.

And I want to say to them, "You have got to be kidding me, right? You do have to say it. She/he can never hear it enough."

We can never hear it enough, and we can't say it enough. *I love you* are the three most powerful words we could ever know, and God proved that in bringing his son Jesus Christ into our midst, showing us what love looks like physically.

When Susan and I were first married, she would say to me over and over, "Do you love me?" And I'd say back, "Yes, I love you." "Well, tell me that you love me." "Well, I love you." And she would ask me that question over and over. And I finally got kind of fed up with it one day, and I said, "You know, I don't get it. I married you, didn't I? Why is this such a big deal for you?" And she said, "Listen, John, I know that you love me. I want to know that you love me."

Many times since then, I've said, "Susan, do you love me? If you do, tell me that you love me." "Oh, John, you know I love you. I married you, didn't I?" "Oh, Susan, I know you love me. I just want to know you love me." All of us need that, want that, crave that desire to be loved.

Jesus said shortly before he ascended to the Father, "This commandment I leave with you, that you love one another, and people will know if you love one another that you are my disciples."

It's on us to make that happen, in the world in which we live today, where expressing love oftentimes seems to have been lost; instead, vitriolic language or hateful speech or bigoted words seem to be the way we communicate through social media or even just face-to-face. What's happening in the world when love is diminished or depleted or removed altogether? It becomes a cesspool of nastiness.

And the only thing that will clean it out is for us to express our love one to the other over and over again.

We know it's in the political world, and we know it's even in the church. With all that the churches have been going through for any denomination over the last few years, we have seen time and again, on every side of whatever the respective issue may be, nasty, ugly talk. Anything but love. So, it's on us to be a people who find a way to love, to express love, to show love, to be love.

As I've said before, when I was in high school and in college, I worked in nursing homes. I was an orderly. I did all the dirty work, and I loved my job. I loved being around elderly people, mostly women, because all the husbands were already gone. And I enjoyed listening to them talk about everyday life, just getting to know them.

But there was one woman there who was in a room by herself, who was not an elderly woman by any means. I would guess, though I was in my early twenties (and not very sure of the age of anybody over twenty-two), that she was somewhere around forty. She was in a semi-comatose state in a single room, and she just lay in the bed day after day looking at the ceiling with no focus in her eyes and no movement in her body.

When I first started working there, the nurses said to me, "Well, listen, she's unresponsive and has no understanding of her surroundings or knows anything. But you're going to have to go in, attend to her, and you're going to have to change her sheets and get her in a wheelchair. Sadly, she's going to be completely unresponsive in every way. Just be aware of that."

The very first day I went into her room for whatever reason; maybe I had forgotten that she was "unresponsive." I don't remember, but I started talking to her as I did anybody else, going about my orderly business. "Hey, how's the day been? I want to tell you about my day." For many days afterward I just went through that same routine. And I would talk to her while I was bathing and changing her and the sheets and doing all that needed to be done to make her more comfortable and her room as presentable as possible. And I would tell her, "I sure do like your hair" and make other small talk.

And then one day I walked in, and before I said another word, she turned her head and looked at me, her eyes completely focused. The rest of the time I worked there, she could never speak, she couldn't move on her own, but she could move her head. She knew what was going on because she was responsive to love. How long had she gone without any kind of love because she didn't matter, she didn't know anything, and maybe nobody spoke to her? But, over time, as love and care were expressed, she responded.

I hope you'll say those special three words of affection to each other over and over again. Then you're going to discover you can't say it enough and you can't hear it enough. We all need it.

"Love never ends," says Paul.

It doesn't insist on its own way. Love is always concerned about someone else. So, maybe I don't say it enough. I'm going to really work on saying it a lot more, and I'm going to say it to you. To those whom I love, I love you.

Hallelujah. Amen.

Leading by Following

> *The king of Egypt said to the Hebrew midwives, one of whom was named Shiphrah and the other Puah, "When you act as midwives to the Hebrew women and see them on the birthstool, if it is a son, kill him, but if it is a daughter, she shall live." But the midwives feared God; they did not do as the king of Egypt commanded them, but they let the boys live. So, the king of Egypt summoned the midwives and said to them, "Why have you done this and allowed the boys to live?" The midwives said to Pharaoh, "Because the Hebrew women are not like the Egyptian women, for they are vigorous and give birth before the midwife comes to them." So, God dealt well with the midwives, and the people multiplied and became very strong. And because the midwives feared God, he gave them families.*
>
> —EXODUS 1:5–21

I know a lot about finishing in second place. When I was in junior high, I played the snare drum in the band for one year. The band director came up to me one day and said, "John, you are the second best snare drum player in the band." Now, normally that would be a compliment, but there were only two snare drum players in the band.

When I was in junior high, I wrestled. And one year, my record was flawless. I was undefeated, and I was wrestling for the city championship in Fort Worth, Texas. I was going to finish the year undefeated, but in my last match of the year I was defeated, and I finished in second place.

I'm familiar with second place. Years went by. I was serving a little church in Fort Worth that grew rapidly. We grew so successfully and rapidly that someone nominated me for a national award that, by the way, no longer exists, but at the time it was called the Circuit Rider Award given by the United Methodist Publishing House. I finished runner-up for the award.

I'm comfortable with second place, but I'm not satisfied with second place. But there are those who understand their role being second really in a variety of ways means that they are first. Think about supporting actors, for example. They don't get top billing. They don't have the primary role. They're not the main character, but oftentimes supporting actors are the ones who carry the movie or the play.

A few years ago, Susan and I went to Broadway to see a musical, and we were looking forward to seeing the lead actor who was starring in the musical. However, as we stood in line to go in, we were informed that he was not going to be on stage that night, but the understudy was. I'd never heard of the understudy. I was so disappointed. We paid all that money. I pouted and told Susan, "I don't want to go after all." She said, "As much as we paid for these tickets, get in there and sit down and be quiet." And the understudy, the one who oftentimes gets second billing or lower, was extraordinarily good. I was so glad we went after all.

There are times when people who seem to have a lesser role in a variety of ways really shine if they are given a chance to prove themselves in the overall saga. In other words, they lead by following the opportunity.

Shiphrah and Puah were two Hebrew midwives who helped women give birth. A long time ago, the Hebrews, the Israelite people, were held captive in Egypt, and they were growing exponentially while there. Pharaoh, however, began to be threatened by the tremendous growth of the Israelite population in his midst and became fearful that they would try to overthrow him.

So Pharaoh set out a mandate that all Hebrew boys, as they were being born into the world, were to be put to death. The girls could live, but the boys were to be no more.

Shiphrah and Puah got a word from God, saying, "You spare the boys." And so, of course, they did. They allowed the boys to live. When Pharaoh got wind that Hebrew boys were still being born into the world, he confronted Shiphrah and Puah, and the women came up with an elaborate story. They told the Pharaoh that those Hebrew women were not like Egyptian women. When Hebrew women were going to have a baby, by golly, they had a baby. By that they meant, by the time they got to the mothers, it was too late. The babies had already been born into the world.

Shiphrah and Puah led by following God's word, by following God's instruction. They became leaders. They didn't intend to be leaders. They weren't seeking that role. They were simply being faithful to what it was they were called to do. But in the process of doing so, they spared the lives of many Hebrew boys and certainly kept a lot of Hebrew mothers from grieving deeply.

But even more importantly than that, these two women, by following God's lead, started the process that would eventually lead to the birth of Moses and, finally and fundamentally, to the liberation of the Israelite people years later.

Oftentimes, because of the culture in which we live, people who are in positions of authority or people who are in the spotlight get more blame and more accolades than maybe they deserve. But more often than not, people who are in a position to receive those accolades or blame are often heavily reliant on those who are behind the scenes to do her or his part to make a difference. And real leaders are often the kinds of individuals in the Christian faith who follow first. Sometimes we are followers who are not all supposed to be leaders. We already have a leader in Jesus.

For years in the United Methodist Church and other denominations, being a leader was oftentimes expected because there were so many workshops and books written about subjects like, *How to be a leader, How to be a confident leader*; and *How to lead the charge*. These workshops and books were about taking the lead, being in charge, stepping up, leading the troops. And the truth of the matter is, I wished over the years that we didn't have workshops on how to be a leader but instead on how to be a follower—because we already have a leader in Jesus Christ.

Not everybody needs to be out front. We have the one who is always supposed to be out front, and we lead first by following him, following his instruction, following his mandates for our lives, following his example, and in doing so, we then lead other people into a right relationship with God. We lead by following.

Remember what Jesus did. He prayed, and then he went out to seek his disciples, to handpick his disciples. And when he handpicked each disciple, he said to them, "Come and follow me." Jesus didn't say, "Come and be the leader."

Jesus said, "Come and follow me." He later told those who followed him, "Take up your cross and follow me."

In the Gospel of John, Jesus said, "I am the Good Shepherd, and you are the sheep, and the sheep follow me because they know my voice." We have the leader. Our responsibility is to follow that leader, and when we follow that leader, we lead the charge in what it means to be the kind of people who make a fundamental yet powerful difference in the world.

By following the Prince of Peace, we help establish peace. By following the bread of life, we help feed the hungry. By following the one who said, "Any time you clothe someone who is naked, you clothe me," we do what is necessary to provide for the needs of others. In following the one who is the leader, we step up and take the lead in the world when we are void of leadership in so many ways.

What was extraordinary about Shiphrah and Puah was that they were just doing what they were supposed to be doing and never deviated from it. Even when Pharaoh said, "You do what I tell you to do," they didn't bow down before Pharaoh. They always remained faithful, bowing down before God and God's instruction. Shiphrah and Puah used love and life to fight evil and death. It's interesting to me to think about the impact they made in sparing these little newborn baby boys. One was Moses who, years later with God's help, would free the Israelites who had been enslaved by Pharaoh. If those women had not done their part there would have been no Moses, and there would have likely been no liberation of the Israelite people.

What makes this story extraordinary is that to this day we know the names of the two midwives and these

115

behind-the-scenes figures. We have no earthly idea the name of Pharaoh. These two women became leaders simply by following.

In the Civil War, there was a major general by the name of John Rawlins. Most of us have heard very little, if anything, about John Rawlins but that he was a supporter of Ulysses S. Grant. In fact, he was Grant's primary support system.

Grant was the one who got all the attention, got all the accolades, and was considered the great leader of the Union Army. But that wasn't really the case in many ways. You see, Ulysses S. Grant had a major drinking problem. He got drunk regularly, and sometimes he was drunk at the most inappropriate of times when he should have been leading his men.

Major General Rawlins finally persuaded General Grant to try to stay sober. In fact, he made Grant swear that he would try to remain sober. Grant oftentimes succeeded, and on other occasions he fell woefully short. When the latter occurred, it was Rawlins who stepped up and took the lead. And eventually, because of his support for Grant, Grant was able to pick himself up again and lead his troops. We read a lot about Ulysses S. Grant, but his support system enabled his work to be continued by someone who was in a supporting role, if you will. That man was someone who was behind the scenes but who made an extraordinary difference. And eventually, the Union Army persevered in winning the Civil War. Rawlins was a leader, but he knew what he had to do in following Grant.

It is extraordinary to think about how necessary it is for all of us to lead but first lead by following. As Christians, we have a leader. Our job is to follow the leader, and naturally, leadership takes over when we follow first.

I read an interesting story some time ago that in 1943, the Nazis decided to round up the Jews in Italy. There weren't a lot of Jews in Italy, but there were Jews, and in the minds of the Nazis, they needed to be eliminated. So the Nazi soldiers came into Rome and began to round up Jews. At the same time, there was suddenly this new, deadly disease that the Nazis heard about that was spreading among the Jews.

This strange new affliction was called Syndrome K, and if one contracted Syndrome K, she or he would begin to cough, and after coughing for a while, eventually they would become paralyzed, and then their lungs would be paralyzed, and they would die. It was a serious infection, and it was working its way for whatever reason throughout the Jewish community. As a result, the Nazi soldiers began to back off.

As some of the soldiers went to the hospital to round up some of these Jews, the hospital administration warned them of the need to be careful. When they searched the hallways, the patients were critically ill. And as a few of the soldiers bravely went in and heard all these Jewish people coughing hysterically and writhing in pain, the Nazi regiment quickly fled through the hospital doors. And they gave up rounding up these Jews that were in the hospital, more than a hundred of them. They left them alone.

But here's what's fascinating. There was no such thing as Syndrome K. It was made up by the lead physician in the hospital, Dr. Giovanni Borromeo. He thought to himself that there had to be some way to protect these Jews who were in the hospital. They didn't need to be in the hospital because they were not sick, but that's where they were placed for protection. And when the German soldiers would walk down the hall, the physicians instructed everybody to cough as loud as they could and to moan as much as they could. And the soldiers left.

After the war, Borromeo was notably honored by the Italian government. And years later, posthumously, he was honored by the Israeli government for sparing the lives of Jewish people who otherwise would have been put to death. Now, he didn't do it for the acclaim. He didn't do it for the attention. He did it because he was following his faith. He was following what he knew he should be doing to protect other human beings. And in following, he led the charge, and lots of people were protected.

I hope you'll think about what you can resolve to do to be a follower of Jesus Christ. And know that when you do that, in following him, you ultimately will lead. You will lead other people to Jesus Christ. You will lead other people to take responsibility for their faith and to make a difference in the world. You will lead people toward peace and wholeness and reconciliation and forgiveness. You will lead them toward grace personified in the one we bow down before.

Each year ahead we are going to have opportunities to make a difference.

We're going to lead, but we're going to lead by following him.

Hallelujah. Amen.

If at First
You Don't Succeed

> They came to Bethsaida. Some people brought a blind man to him and begged him to touch him. He took the blind man by the hand and led him out of the village, and when he had put saliva on his eyes and laid his hands on him, he asked him, "Can you see anything?" And the man looked up and said, "I can see people, but they look like trees, walking." Then Jesus laid his hands on his eyes again, and he looked intently, and his sight was restored, and he saw everything clearly. Then he sent him away to his home, saying, "Do not even go into the village."
>
> —MARK 8:22–26

We don't get really excited about "ALMOSTS". We don't tend to celebrate people who almost accomplish something. History books are not riddled with the names of people who almost climbed Mount Everest. We don't throw a party for someone who almost passed the bar. And the church cannot do the work we are called to do when people almost contribute financially in support of the mission and ministry of our congregation.

We tend to celebrate great accomplishments and achievements where the causes and goals have been reached. We don't get excited about "almosts". Can you imagine what it would be like if we almost won the Second

World War? What would you think if you found out the one who was about to perform your surgery almost graduated from medical school? And what would the world be like if those women who went to the tomb and looked in and saw an empty tomb had almost told the world that he had risen?

We don't get particularly excited about "almosts". But there are times when "almosts" keep us going when we're almost there. If we believe that we almost had a cure for cancer, we will keep fighting and trying and funding so that we will reach the goal of no more cancer. If we could almost eradicate poverty and hunger across the world so that no one ever went without, we would continue to make every effort. There are times when "almosts" keep us motivated, keep us encouraged, keep us on the right path.

Mark tells us an extraordinary story that is only recorded in his gospel about how Jesus almost healed someone. At first, he didn't succeed, but he tried again. People brought a blind man to Jesus. We discover that his sight will be restored, which means of course that at one time he could see. We don't know his name, and we don't know the condition that he has that caused him to lose his eyesight. But he has friends who bring him to Jesus and ask Jesus to do something. It is obvious that they want their friend's eyesight to be restored.

Jesus ended up taking him outside the city gates. This was highly unusual, for Jesus didn't usually do that when he had an encounter with someone in the moment. But on this occasion, he took the blind man by the hand and led him outside the city limits and used everything in his arsenal. He touched the man. He even used his own spittle to touch the eyes of the man who was blind. Then Jesus, as if he already knew, said to the blind man, "Can you see?" To which the blind man said, "Well, I can see people, but they're like trees." In other words, his sight had not been fully restored, and Jesus had to do it again.

Now, why would Mark include this story in his gospel? If I were putting together Mark's epistle, I probably would have left this one out. I know what it's like to be in the condition of the young man who lost his eyesight. When I was in high school, I was involved in a terrible work-related construction accident. And as a result, I lost sight in my right eye. It was terribly damaged, and I had to have surgery. Hospitalized for two weeks, I was blind in my eye for an extended period, and every day my mother would have to put this salve on my eye. Where Jesus used spittle, my mother used this salve to keep the eye moist and to bring about some form of healing.

The doctor who performed the surgery said the likelihood of my ever having sight again in that eye was very slim, but I kept doing what the doctor told me to do. At one point they told me, "Whatever you do, don't take that patch off your eye. It helps with the healing process." Being a fifteen-year-old, I decided I knew more than the doctor did, so I'd just take the patch off when I chose to, because I wanted to be able to see so desperately out of this injured eye. For a long time I couldn't.

Finally, one day I uncovered my bad eye and covered my good eye and saw a flicker on the television. I was over the moon excited! And as my eyesight began to come back I noticed people. And do you know what they looked like? Trees! I'd see a trunk and then see branches. I was so taken with this story because what this blind man said was absolutely true. He kind of had his eyesight restored, and at that point I kind of had my eyesight restored. Now, as the years have passed by, I have pretty good eyesight. I need to wear glasses, but I can see that I'm very fortunate and very, very blessed.

Why would Mark include this story? Why in the world did it take Jesus two times to bring about total healing for someone who was blind? If you read the Gospel of Mark, you discover something that makes it stand out from the other gospels. In Mark's gospel, Jesus is continually surrounded by unbelief, by a lack of belief not only on the part of the community at large but even his closest companions.

Evidently in Mark's gospel Jesus is highly reliant on the faith of those around him to bring about healing. In Mark's gospel the disciples never get it. Those twelve hand-selected intimate friends of Jesus who were following him everywhere and listening to all his teachings and his preaching and seeing one miracle performed after another never really understand for themselves who Jesus is.

You remember the occasion where Jesus is in a boat with the disciples and there is a storm that is raging? Jesus calms the seas, and the first thing the disciples do is look at each other and say, "Who is this guy that he could do something like this now?" He is well into his ministry by this time. They've seen him do all kinds of things. What did they mean? "Who is this guy?" They just didn't understand, and their unbelief seemed to take a toll on Jesus's capacity to bring about healing on occasion in Mark's gospel.

Jesus's own family—his siblings and even his mother in Mark's gospel—said to those who were closest to Jesus,

"He's out of his mind!" They seemed to indicate that he had lost his way and that his own family did not understand who he was. He was just inundated with a lack of belief on the part of those he was trying to minister to. And the fatigue of that—emotionally, physically, and spiritually—evidently took a toll on Jesus and his capacity to do what he was more than capable of doing.

Just preceding this story, Jesus turned to those who were around him in total frustration and asked, "Are your hearts still hardened? Do your eyes still fail to see, and your ears still fail to hear? Do you still not understand?" One can sense and feel the exhaustion on the part of Jesus in Mark's gospel moreso than any of the others when it comes to the frustration of his respective audiences not being able to fully appreciate who Jesus is.

But if at first you don't succeed you try again, and that's just what Jesus did. He didn't say to the young man, "I gave you my best shot. You can see better now than you could before—maybe not fully, but you can at least see trees walking around better. You okay with that, going about your business?" But Jesus didn't do that. He did what he was supposed to do, and he completed the task even if it took him a second effort, but he did it. There!

Are there times when Jesus could have easily quit and he didn't? If at first you don't succeed, you try again. You don't quit on people, and Jesus never quit on anyone. There were those occasions when he was given ample opportunity to do so, but he didn't. There were even times when Jesus wanted to quit.

Remember when Jesus was in the Garden of Gethsemane? He said to the disciples, "Please just pray. I'm going to go off by myself and pray." And the disciples fell asleep. They couldn't even stay awake when Jesus is in a desperate state. And scripture tells us that as Jesus prayed, his sweat was like great drops of blood, and he said to God, "Let this cup pass from me. I don't want to go through this. I know what's about to happen to me! I'm going to be brutalized! I'm going to be tortured! I'm going be killed!" And Jesus could have walked away.

But he didn't. He said, "Father, it's not my will; it's your will. This is your decision, and I'm going to abide by that." He didn't quit on us. If he had quit in the garden, there would have been no cross. And there would have been, of course, no resurrection.

But Jesus, even though there was a part of him that longed to do so, he never quit on us. He completed his task. He fulfilled his responsibility. Do you remember when he was hanging on the cross and people were spitting on him and mocking him and laughing at him? And there were those who said, "If you are who you claim to be, come on down from the cross." In that moment Jesus could have quit. He wasn't dead yet. They hadn't killed him yet. They brutalized him, but he was still alive. He could have come down from the cross and gone about his way. But he had not completed his task. He had not taken upon himself all the sin of all humanity for all time and died to that sin.

So, he didn't come down. He didn't quit, and as a result of not quitting, we recognize of course that my sin and your sin are no longer our sin. It became a part of who Jesus is and was. As the apostle Paul said, he became sin who knew no sin for the sake of all of humanity.

He didn't quit when that would have been the easy thing to do. And I wrestle continually with the notion that if I were the writer of the Gospel of Mark, would I have included this story? At some level it almost makes Jesus look weak. But on the contrary, I think what it really does is remind us of who Jesus is and our responsibility to be a people who believe that when we trust in the One we call the Christ, we are energized and motivated and encouraged to believe that our belief makes a difference.

And we too are called just like Jesus to recognize those moments in life when we try to accomplish something, we try to fulfill a goal. We try to reach something that we've always wanted to reach, and we fall short. The easy thing to do is quit, but we remind ourselves like Jesus, if at first you don't succeed, you don't quit. You try again!

Have you ever just felt the total absence of God? Have you ever been in a place spiritually where there is this void, this sense of emptiness? You don't quit on God in moments like that. What you do is, you try again.

Have you ever in your life had some kind of obstacle that you can't seem to shake? You can't seem to get rid of it, can't seem to overcome it? You don't give into it and just say, "I've got to deal with it." You keep trying, you keep working. If at first you don't succeed, you try again.

Have you ever read your Bible, regularly prayed daily, worshiped weekly, and still felt nothing? You don't give up. You don't say well, that was a total waste of time. You keep trying. If at first you don't succeed, you take the example of Jesus and you try again. You keep going; you keep doing it; you fulfill what you're supposed to do and who you're supposed to be.

All of us at one time or another in life have reached a point where we've said, "Enough is enough. I quit." We've all done that. We've quit on relationships. We've quit on responsibilities. We've all been there. But fundamentally and finally, our responsibility is to be bigger than that. We must live above all that and use the example that we have in Jesus about how we're supposed to be who God calls us to be.

The Barna Group is a very credible research organization that continually puts out information that's readily available to all of us and extraordinarily helpful. In interviewing many clergypersons in January of 2021, they found that 29 percent of all clergy, male and female, across all denominations and nondenominational churches, said that they were seriously contemplating quitting ministry. Later, in March of 2022, that number had risen to 43 percent. So more than four out of every ten clergy that you ever meet are seriously considering leaving active ministry for good.

The Barna Group tried to discover why it is that so many of these clergy are ready to leave ministry. Apparently, the number one reason is the intense and overwhelming pressure of trying to get people to come back after the COVID pandemic, combined with a lackluster attitude about the church trying to raise money continually to keep people employed to do the work the clergy are called to do. The second reason is the intense and profound sense of isolation and loneliness that accompanies the job. I as clergy can sympathize with both of those reasons that prevailed in the survey.

Then, when asked, "Why are you still doing it if you're contemplating leaving it?" the overwhelming response clergy gave was, "Because I was called to do it. It's not my choice." I think for all of us, we reach a point in life where there may be occasions when we need to quit. It's either time to move on or whatever it may be. But when it comes to the faith, when it comes to trying to be who we're called to be—even in those moments in life where we are spiritually empty, even on those occasions when we'd rather do something else than come to church—our responsibility is to keep doing it. And when we don't feel like we think we ought to feel, we still don't quit. We don't give up. If at first you don't succeed, you keep plugging away. You keep trying. You keep going at it. It's got to happen. It must, because it's true. If at first you don't succeed, you try again. You simply just keep plugging away.

There is a woman who is a schoolteacher. She arrives early every morning, and as her day progresses, she must deal with an administrative staff that's not really interested in her or her classroom. She has a lot of disinterested students, many of whom have parents who are constantly complaining. She stays up late every single night grading all those papers, until she finally reaches a point where she says that enough is enough. "They don't pay me enough! The hours are too long! I'm worn out, and I quit!" But the next morning, she arrives at the school early and goes through the routine all over again.

And then there is the couple that squabbles all the time. They just continually fight about everything. They fight over money. They fight over how to discipline their children. They fight over the big things, the medium things, and especially over the pettiest of things. They simply have gotten to a place in their relationship with each other where they don't like one another anymore.

127

Finally, one evening, in a very rational way, they sit down and they say to one another that it's time to quit. It's over. They go to bed. They wake up the next morning, and, before they go to their respective places of work, they kiss one another, and they say, "I love you." All over again.

There is a doctor who's close to retirement. He's worked many years trying to bring about healing. But too many of his patients smoke too much, drink too often, eat very poorly, and get little to no exercise, and it frustrates him continually. He gives advice daily to people who he knows are not going to take it, not going to comply with his recommendations, and not do what needs to be done to live a full and healthy life.

He works very long hours. His feet are tired every night when he gets home, having made rounds at the hospital once again. Oftentimes, he's been seeing those very people who are patients in the hospital who would never be there to begin with if they had simply done what he had told them to do some time ago.

He goes home one night, and he's had enough. He's close enough to retirement maybe to make it financially. Though he's not quite ready, he still thinks he's had enough. Then he argues with himself that he's ready to quit, and he declares, "I'm done! No more!" And the next day, he knocks on the first examining room door, walks in, says good morning to his patient and asks, "How are you feeling?" All over again.

Isn't that what life is like for a lot of us? We have "almost" experiences regularly. We almost got what we wanted. We almost made it. We almost reached the goal. We almost quit. But there's something deep down inside of us that says, "If at first you don't succeed …" And we keep try-ing. We keep doing our part. Just like Jesus, we don't quit.

Hallelujah. Amen.

Marked *and* *Claimed*

> So, John the baptizer appeared in the wilderness, proclaiming a baptism of repentance for the forgiveness of sins. And the whole Judean region and all the people of Jerusalem were going out to him and were baptized by him in the River Jordan, confessing their sins. Now John was clothed with camel's hair, with a leather belt around his waist, and he ate locusts and wild honey. He proclaimed, "The one who is more powerful than I is coming after me; I am not worthy to stoop down and untie the strap of his sandals. I have baptized you with water, but he will baptize you with the Holy Spirit." In those days Jesus came from Nazareth of Galilee and was baptized by John in the Jordan. And just as he was coming up out of the water, he saw the heavens torn apart and the Spirit descending like a dove upon him. And a voice came from the heavens, "You are my Son, the Beloved; with you I am well pleased."
>
> —MARK 1:4–11

Early in our marriage, Susan and I saved up our money and went to an upscale white-tablecloth restaurant to celebrate something important. Maybe it was our anniversary. It's been so long ago I am not sure, but we were excited about the chance to go to this restaurant, be greeted by a maître d', be seated at a beautifully decorated table, look over a very elegant (yet expensive) menu, and have a wonderful time together.

It started out that way, and we were really enjoying one another's company. It was nice to be together, when suddenly the restaurant's front door flung open, and these loud and boisterous men stormed in. Most activity in the room came to a standstill as all eyes turned to the entrance.

I recognized one of the guys right away. He was a sportscaster, famous across the nation and even the world. And he was the loudest of all, as he and his group of men made their way back to a room at the far end of the restaurant away from us, with the volume only getting louder. I was intrigued, knowing who this person was. Even Susan knew of him as did most everybody in the restaurant.

Though he'd been obnoxiously loud, I thought this might be the only chance I'd ever have to get his autograph. So I encouraged the maître d' to come over and asked, "Listen, is it all right to go to that back room to get his autograph?" But he advised me in a very sophisticated way, "You wouldn't want to do that. He's a drunk and jerk"—but he used a word other than "jerk".

So I remained seated. Though the drunks were behind closed doors of the far room the whole time we were there, all the diners in the restaurant could still hear their loud, disrespectful conduct driven by too much alcohol. I read some time later that this same sportscaster entered an alcohol rehab clinic where he discovered sobriety. He then started attending a church, where he gave his life to Jesus Christ and was baptized.

In an interview shortly after his baptism he stated, "What baptism does is it gives me a sense of what I am and to whom I belong. And the moment I knew that, I felt like a forty-pound weight had been lifted off my shoulders."

This sportscaster passed on a few years later. I found his to be a fascinating story about his conversion experience and what baptism meant for him.

Jesus was baptized by John the Baptizer in the River Jordan. In the Gospel of Luke, he waited in line with everybody else to be baptized. Mark was very succinct with what he said, but John baptized him. In that moment Jesus was baptized. The Holy Spirit descended as if it were a dove and said, "This is my son, the beloved, with whom I am well pleased." But why was Jesus baptized? He was without sin.

And why do United Methodists emphasize baptism? In fact, in order for one to be a member of a respective congregation, she or he must be baptized. And if they haven't been baptized, then we baptize her or him. In the United Methodist Church, we recognize anyone's baptism from any Christian denomination. So most times, when people unite with our congregation from another denomination, we don't baptize them if they've already been baptized. As far as United Methodism is concerned, they've already been marked and claimed by God.

So why was Jesus baptized? And why do United Methodists put emphasis on baptism as a sacrament, a holy sacred act? Well, there are three primary reasons why Jesus was baptized, and all three of those reasons go hand in hand with our recognition of the importance of baptism.

The first reason Jesus was baptized is that it was a sign of solidarity with all of humanity. If you look in the scriptures, Jesus never asked his followers to do anything that he was unwilling to do himself. Remember how Jesus said,

"You must forgive" seventy times seven. We know that on the cross, Jesus took upon himself all the sin of all humanity and died to that sin. And remember what he said: "Father, forgive them, for they know not what they do." Jesus was one who lived forgiveness even as he breathed his last. Our baptism is a sign of solidarity with Jesus, that we are one with Christ. He became baptized, a sign of solidarity, that he is one with us.

Secondly, it's also a public declaration. When Jesus was baptized, the Holy Spirit descended and said, "This is my beloved, with whom I am well pleased." In that moment, it was a public declaration at Jesus's baptism about who he was and is. We believe that our baptism is a public declaration of who *we* are. In that special way, God said to the one being baptized, "You are my son. With you I am well pleased." And the water placed on a child's head is like a brand or mark. It never goes away. In that moment, you're claimed by God. It is a public declaration of who you are in the eyes of God. It was for Jesus. It is for us.

And the third reason is that Jesus was baptized to mark the beginning of his active ministry. Remember, scripture tells us that Jesus was approximately thirty years of age before he began his ministry—that is, before he actually went out and publicly declared who he was. We believe that our baptism is our public event that marks the beginning of our entrance into the ministry of the body of Christ, the church. So, for Jesus, it was a sign of solidarity. It was a public declaration. And it marked the beginning of his ministry.

And we believe, for those three reasons are why we are baptized as well. William Willimon said that baptism just fundamentally asserts who we are and to whom it is we belong. And that's absolutely true. We believe today that in baptism in that moment, God says, "I want everybody to know." That's why we do it publicly. And as God would say, "I want everyone to know this child, this adult, this teenager is mine. And I'm marking them and claiming them as my very own. And I want everybody to know it." That's why United Methodists baptize.

You may remember when King Charles III had his coronation to begin his reign over the United Kingdom. I got up at half past three in the morning to watch it, because as I've told you before, I've desperately wanted to be royalty, but, as a commoner, must live vicariously through real royalty. But I did get up early to watch Charles's coronation, with Susan arising soon afterward, and we watched every single bit of it.

Now, here's the fundamental question: why did they have to have a coronation? Because the truth is, the moment Queen Elizabeth died, he went from Prince Charles to King Charles III. The coronation was months later. Why did they have to have a coronation? He was already king. Because the coronation is a public display of who he is and his role in the world.

That's what happens to us in baptism. We already know that we belong to God. We already know that we're claimed by God. So why do we baptize? Because it is a public display of who we are and our role in the church. And if we're too young to answer for ourselves, then it's on Mom and Dad and the family and the church together to teach that child, so that she or he one day will claim it for themselves. But no matter what happens, they're marked by God. They're claimed by God in baptism, and they're never the same as a result.

You know, one of the reasons we ask the parents, "Mom, Dad, what name is given this child?"—and we say the first and middle name—is because they take on a new name. They have the name that Mom and Dad gave her or him, but they take on a new name called *Christian*, which means they're never the same.

They're marked and claimed, and everybody gets to know it. And in that moment, God says, "You're my child, the beloved. With you I am well pleased." And now the baptized person's role is to be a part of the life of the body of Christ itself. It is our sign of solidarity with Jesus Christ. It is a public declaration of who we are, and that never changes. And I think that's so important for all of us to remember in life, in general.

Remember, we do not rebaptize. I told you earlier that if one joins our congregation from another church and that individual has been baptized, we do not rebaptize. Because we believe in that moment it was God who claimed that person. It is God who marked that person. We simply acknowledge what God has always done and will always do in that person's life. So if we were to rebaptize, it would be like saying, "God didn't take the first time. We have to do it all over." We don't believe that. In fact, the book of Ephesians says in the fourth chapter, "There's one Lord, one faith, one baptism."

I know people who claim to have been baptized many times. Every time something sinful happens, they feel they must be baptized again. Scripture is clear. It's a one-time event, because we believe it's what God is doing in the individual's life that is so incredibly important. And as United Methodist Christians, we believe that everybody needs to be a part of that experience as much as possible. So we don't rebaptize.

We also, in the United Methodist tradition, recognize three forms of baptism—either sprinkling, immersion, or pouring, which is oftentimes what the Roman Catholics do. In the early days of the church, when they started having structures where people gathered together, oftentimes there was not a source of water close by. Therefore, in the church, they started participating in different forms of baptism, pouring or sprinkling or immersion. In the United Methodist Church, we recognize all three, and we can do all three. I've done all three before, many times. So people will say sometimes, "Well, it doesn't count if they weren't fully immersed because you didn't do it like Jesus did it." And I want to remind you, if we're going to be strict about the law, that means that everybody who ever intends to be baptized has to be baptized by a guy who ate locusts, and we have to do it in the Jordan River.

Obviously, one accommodates the circumstances to the situation. The church has always recognized those three forms. Does immersion count? Of course it does. You ask anybody who's been immersed, they'll tell you it counts. I've done it in swimming pools. I have baptized people who were minutes away from death in a hospital bed.

God knows what's going on, and God is the one in charge of all that takes place in baptism. We are simply doing what we believe God has already done in an individual's life in a sacred and holy way to acknowledge it. Sometimes I will have someone, particularly with young confirmands who may have been baptized as a child or as an infant, who will come and say, "Well, my friends at school said my baptism doesn't count, because when I was three months old they sprinkled water on my head, and so it doesn't count." And I always say, "Oh yes, it does, it counts. You've been baptized. You've been marked by God and claimed by God, and you can try and scrub it off. But, it's not going to come off. It's on there forever. You belong to God, and that's what baptism is for us."

So, remember, this is important. We are not christening. We are baptizing. A lot of people call the church and say, "We would like to schedule our child to be christened in the church." To christen is to name something or someone, like a ship, for example. They christened the *Queen Mary* ocean liner. But generally, we don't do that with people in the United Methodist Church. In fact, I've never been a part of a service like that, but I've been a part of hundreds of baptisms because of what baptisms proclaim.

Christening is to name. Baptism is to proclaim who one is and who one belongs to. Because remember, Jesus said in the Gospel of John, "You didn't choose me. I chose you." That means we belong to Jesus. He's already claimed us as his very own. That's what our baptism does for us. The apostle Paul says, "You are not your own. You have been bought with a price. You're not your own. You belong to God."

We see in scripture time and again, from the mouth of our Savior and from the greatest apostle, that we belong to someone else. We belong to our God we know in and through Jesus Christ, and baptism is a public display of that. Now, if one is baptized as an adult, certainly she or he acknowledges their sin in baptism and that they are a new creation in Christ Jesus in that moment. But that's also why age is irrelevant for us. Because remember, it's about what God's doing in the moment, not what we have done or are doing. So that's why we, like millions of other Christians across the world, will baptize babies. They don't have any idea what's going on, but I can tell you I've baptized many adults who have no earthly idea what's going on either.

You just fundamentally need to believe that, in the life of the church, God knows what we're doing and why we're doing it, and it's the meaning over the method. And I think that's very important.

It's also important for us to remember that baptism is that moment in life where we belong to God, and it is a public announcement that we belong to God. And we know God in and through Jesus Christ, and we have an obligation to tell everyone about that from the moment we're baptized. We have the capability to tell others about it from then on. In other words, we're never the same after baptism. Even if we don't really understand what's going on, the Holy Spirit certainly does, and the Holy Spirit's working in and through us in a powerful way.

We have what we call prevenient grace, which is God's love for us from the moment we're conceived. And that prevenient grace is evident in baptism. That's important for us because we're changed. We're a new creation. You said, "Jesus, I chose you." And God said, "You belong to me. Your baptism shows that to the world."

I read an article some time ago about a young African teenage girl who came to a church one day to be baptized. Her family was made up of nonbelievers. When she came forward for baptism, the pastor who was to baptize her noticed that she had brought her luggage, which was sitting in another corner of the church.

The pastor asked her, "Why did you bring your luggage with you to the baptism?" And she said, "Because my dad told me this morning that if I go to that Christian church and I'm baptized, I am to never come home again. So I brought my luggage with me."

See, she understood, just like her unbelieving dad, that the moment she was baptized, she'd change. She'd never be the same. Even her unbelieving dad knew that was going to happen.

We in the church take baptism very seriously. It's very important to us. That's why it is a sacrament in the Protestant church, that we participate in the sacrament of baptism.

When I was in another church, there was a couple who lived close to us who joined our congregation with a beautiful little boy. And when he was about three years of age, they called me and said, "John, we'd like to have our son baptized, and can we schedule a date for the baptism?"

And I said, "Okay, he's three years old. Why don't you do your best to try to explain to him what baptism means?" So on that Sunday morning, they arrived at the church and on his head he was wearing swimming goggles, and he wouldn't take them off before the service started.

His mom kept telling him, "You can take them off now."

And curiously I asked, "But why is he wearing swimming goggles?"

To which she said, "Well, we sat down with him and told him that you were going to put water on his head. And it was very important that that water stay with his head forever and that he needed to know how important it was."

So he wore his goggles. Now, he's probably one of the few people who have ever been baptized wearing swimming goggles. But it was so powerful, because a three-year-old got it. He understood. This was important.

There's going to be water on my head. I'm never going to be who I used to be.

Now, could he articulate all of that? No, but he understood it. A three-year-old understood it. So why do United Methodists baptize?

Because we all need it, and we all need to know it. Because God's the one who said it, we're the ones who spread the word about it, and we're the ones who celebrate it.

That's why we baptize.

Hallelujah. Amen.

Growing *the* Kingdom

The Apple company started in a garage. It became the largest of computer companies, now worth over a trillion dollars. Amazon started as an online bookstore, and in its first few years of existence it did not turn a profit. And now the CEO of Amazon is worth billions of dollars. And the company itself is worth hundreds of billions of dollars. The telephone was invented in 1876. Only the wealthiest of the wealthy could even imagine having something like that in their homes back then. And now we all carry one with us, everywhere we go, the capacity to communicate with anyone, anywhere, at any time. The telephone certainly has evolved.

All those businesses, those inventions, started small. And now they have grown into something enormous, something that, quite frankly, many of us can no longer imagine living without. What would it be like to live without our cell phones? Oh, we can only imagine the joy, right? Small things sometimes emerge into life-changing opportunities. Jesus told us a parable, a parable about a mustard seed that was small but, when planted and nurtured, could grow into a great big shrub.

He also told us about a little bit of yeast mixed with the right ingredients that could produce a staggering amount for people to eat. Those things that are small, said Jesus, with God's help, can do the most extraordinary things to benefit the rest of us.

Think about it for a moment. There are things in life that we experience that are very small to begin with, but we have become the beneficiaries as a result. Think about the church. The book of Acts states that when the church was born into existence, there were only 120 Christians. Now, there are 2.5 billion Christians worldwide. The church started very small; that was an infinitesimal number of people compared to the overall population at the time.

And look what happened as a result through human history. We think about those small things that are so meaningful and so powerful in our own lives, and Jesus said that's what the kingdom of God is like—that pervasive reign of God, the kingdom of heaven, the interchangeable phrases *kingdom of God* and *kingdom of heaven*. Matthew used *kingdom of heaven* when the other gospel writers wrote *kingdom of God*. The reason Matthew used the word *heaven* instead of *God* is because his audience was Jewish, and good Jews believe they did not have the right to utter the name of God. They didn't feel worthy.

So, in Matthew's gospel, Jesus referred to the *kingdom of heaven*. It is interchangeable with the *kingdom of God*. It is something that can be very small, can seem rather inconsequential, but by God's great power it can grow into something that is life-changing for all of humanity. Therefore, we never discount the small things we do as followers of Jesus Christ that can have a profound effect well beyond anything we could possibly imagine.

Now, it's interesting that Jesus would choose a mustard seed and yeast to describe those things that can start small and become great and powerful, because in Jesus's day and time, mustard shrubs were a nuisance. They were not something that people wanted around. They dug them up. They got rid of them. And yet, Jesus said the kingdom of heaven was like a mustard seed that grows into a great shrub.

Jesus talked about yeast, but for good Jews, yeast was a symbol of evil. The book of Leviticus said if you were going to present a food offering to God, do not put yeast in it. Remember what Jesus said: beware of the yeast of the Pharisees. So here was Jesus using two symbols, if you will, of things that were a nuisance, bothersome, burdensome, getting in the way—things that were normally considered unappealing.

And Jesus used those very things that were considered unappealing to say they can do something great and good by the power of God for the sake of the kingdom. They can grow the kingdom. And if you look at Jesus's ministry, oftentimes he took those things or those people who were unattractive or unappealing and used them for great good.

If you read the Gospel of Luke, time and time again Jesus used women as an example of faith. Not that women in Jesus's day and time were unappealing, but women had no power. They didn't have authority. Their job was to take care of their husbands, to have babies.

But Jesus used those very women oftentimes to be an example to everybody else of what faith looked like. A woman with a flow of blood who got rid of everything to come into the presence of Jesus, risking it all. And she was made well. And Jesus said, "Your faith has made you well. You're a daughter of Abraham." There was a woman who washed the feet of Jesus with her hair and her tears. Everybody else was critical because she used a costly ointment. But Jesus said, "You better be like her. She gets it. She is preparing my body for burial. You guys don't understand, but this woman does."

Jesus used children. Remember, in the culture and the day and time in which Jesus lived, children were considered a burden until they were old enough to pitch in and help. They were just an extra burden in a world that was difficult enough. And Jesus said, "I must tell you something. All you adults out there, if you want to be a part of the kingdom of heaven, you've got to be like a child." Children had no power. They didn't have any authority. They were literally and figuratively looked down upon. And Jesus said, "But you've got to be like that if you want to be a part of the kingdom."

Jesus elevated women of ill repute. Remember, there were those self-righteous in society who were standing around going, "*Mmm, mmm, mmm.* Look at Jesus talking to those women." And Jesus said, "Let me tell you something, self-righteous people. These women are going to get to heaven before you do."

Jesus ate with tax collectors. You talk about unappealing. Jesus found a way to take those things or those people who the rest of us might have looked down upon or frowned upon and used them as an example of what it means to be a part of the kingdom—how the kingdom can grow as a result—which means, of course, that all of us then fit in to the capacity to make the kingdom grow.

For those of us who are attractive and those of us who are not particularly attractive; and those of us who are smart and those of us who are not particularly smart; and those of us who have a lot of money and those of us who don't have much—guess what? The kingdom can be about all of us. Jesus told us that *all* of us can play a role in doing something to grow the kingdom of heaven. Even a nasty old shrub, even yeast that has been used in the past to symbolize evil. Even those things can do great good, and that means you can too.

Sometimes the most unappealing of things can be so incredibly important for us. There are those of us who are old enough to remember the days when you actually had to go to the bank to make a deposit. You remember that? You went up to a desk where there were deposit slips and withdrawal slips, and you had to fill them out along with everybody else who was doing the same thing. And do you remember when there was always an ink pen there? You remember that ink pen always had a chain on it? Somehow that ink pen was the ugliest ink pen you can imagine, and there was a chain on it—like most of us would steal it! You remember that, right? Now, let me tell you about that ink pen. Those ink pens were called Skilcraft pens—unattractive, but they worked like a charm.

Skilcraft pens were made by blind people in Wisconsin and North Carolina, and they had to meet strict criteria. A Skilcraft pen had to have enough ink in it to last as if you had drawn with it for an entire mile. A Skilcraft pen had to be able to write upside down. They were used by pilots in airplanes when they lost their way who could use it to navigate with a map upside down. Skilcraft pens had to work in temperatures as low as 40 degrees below zero and as high as 160 degrees Fahrenheit. Skilcraft pens were also made to be used in battle; just in case there needed to be an emergency tracheotomy, you used a Skilcraft pen. Now, who could have imagined this pen that was on the end of a chain that was so unappealing could do the most extraordinary of things and were made intentionally just for those purposes?

You are made intentionally just for that—to do great things that sometimes you may consider small, insignificant, and not that important. But you never know how God is going to use you to grow the kingdom of heaven in the simplest of ways or the most complex of ways and everything in between.

When I was serving a church in Texas, one Sunday we had a young African student show up. He was in school about an hour away. He had never been to a Methodist church before and just decided to get online and find a Methodist church. And lucky for us, he found our church and came that Sunday morning. He didn't look like anybody else. He didn't talk like anybody else. At the end of the service, he appeared quite excited. He came up to me and introduced himself.

I said, "We are so glad to have you here. What can we do for you?" He said, "You've already done it." I said, "What have we done?" He looked me in the eye and said, "People shook my hand. Nobody shakes my hand. But these people here shook my hand, and you shook my hand. It feels so good."

It all started—think about this—it all started when someone shook his hand. *Shook his hand!* You talk about growing the kingdom! It's like a mustard seed—a little bitty thing. It's a handshake. Oh, but it's not a little bitty thing. It grows into something bigger and something bigger and something great and good for the sake of the kingdom of heaven!

Something as small and insignificant as a signature on a peace treaty can stop a war. It's just a signature, but no more death. No more destruction. Something as small as a tiny incision can relieve a staggering amount of pain.

Something as little as a handful of people getting together and holding each other accountable spiritually can create a movement called the Methodist movement that would eventually birth an entire denomination. See? It's not always something big and grand. Sometimes, as Jesus said, it's small. It's unappealing. It's not particularly attractive, but you let God go to work and you do your part, and it is amazing what can happen as a result.

I think sometimes those of us who come to church—and those of us who don't—believe we really don't have that much to offer. We're maybe not theologically trained. We don't like to stand up in front of people and talk. We don't have beautiful singing voices. We don't have some of those things that all these other people seem to have. So, we don't know that God can really use us that much. How do you know? You never know. But this much is true. Everybody qualifies. Everybody is capable, and it doesn't matter what you've done or left undone.

I remember a long time ago I was talking to a woman who was in my church, and she had a son she believed to be a bit wayward. He was then in his mid-twenties, and he had made some poor decisions along the way, but she prayed for him daily. She said, "I just want him to come back. I just want him to come back to the faith." He had grown up in the church and had been an important a part of the church.

Several years went by since she had confided in me about her son when finally, one Sunday, she came to me and said, "I've got to tell you, my prayers have been answered. Something so small has changed my son's life and now he's back!" I asked her what had happened. She said he had gone to a church for whatever reason one Sunday, and in their prayer of confession someone said, "God, for many of us we have left undone what we should have done, and what we shouldn't have done we did. Forgive us."

It was just a small sentence within a prayer of confession in an hour-long service of worship, but that small sentence resonated with him. He connected with it. "You mean there are people around me sitting here worshiping God—as well as singing these hymns and offering these prayers and listening intently—who have really messed up? They did what they shouldn't have done, and what they should have done they didn't do? I want to be a part of something like that!"

Well, guess what? Every church can be just like that. God can use you, and God can use me—and you never know. It could be a handshake, it could be a hug, it could be a hello, it could be tutoring, it could be volunteering, it could be who knows what. But you never know. That small little gift that you give someone else—that you may never even know you give—can be like a mustard seed growing into a great shrub. Or like a little bit of yeast mixed, with the right ingredients, can accomplish great good.

For all of us, Jesus reminds us that what oftentimes may seem inconsequential even in our own lives can have the greatest of consequences for the sake of the kingdom of heaven. We do what we do because we are who we are. We are people who believe in the One who is our Savior, who came into the world and dealt with all kinds of folks that the rest of us frown upon. Those folks are the very ones who became examples of what it means to be faithful followers of Jesus Christ.

So, you hang in there, and you plug away. You keep involving yourself in the life of the church. You keep trying to do the little things and the big things for the sake of the kingdom, and you never know, the results can be extraordinary. We're growing the kingdom. The kingdom needs to grow. It's on us. Stick out a hand. Say good morning. Do something this week intentionally for the greater good of someone else. It will take root. It will produce. It will be life changing.

Hallelujah. Amen.

Between

God and You

When God Calls

Now the boy Samuel was ministering to the Lord under Eli. The word of the Lord was rare in those days; visions were not widespread. At that time Eli, whose eyesight had begun to grow dim so that he could not see, was lying down in his room; the lamp of God had not yet gone out, and Samuel was lying down in the temple of the Lord, where the ark of God was. Then the Lord called, "Samuel! Samuel!" and he said, "Here I am!" and ran to Eli and said, "Here I am, for you called me." But he said, "I did not call; lie down again." So, he went and lay down. The Lord called again, "Samuel!" Samuel got up and went to Eli and said, "Here I am, for you called me." But he said, "I did not call, my son; lie down again." Now Samuel did not yet know the Lord, and the word of the Lord had not yet been revealed to him. The Lord called Samuel again, a third time. And he got up and went to Eli and said, "Here I am, for you called me." Then Eli perceived that the Lord was calling the boy. Therefore, Eli said to Samuel, "Go, lie down, and if he calls you, you shall say, 'Speak, Lord, for your servant is listening.'" So, Samuel went and lay down in his place.

Now the Lord came and stood there, calling as before, "Samuel! Samuel!" And Samuel said, "Speak, for your servant is listening." Then the Lord said to Samuel, "See, I am about to do something in Israel that will make both ears of anyone who hears of it tingle. On that day I will fulfill against Eli all that I have spoken concerning his house, from beginning to end. For I have told him that I am about to punish his house forever for the iniquity that he knew, because his sons were blaspheming God, and he did not restrain them. Therefore, I swear to the house of Eli that the iniquity of Eli's house shall not be expiated by sacrifice or offering forever." Samuel lay there until morning; then he opened the doors of the house of the Lord. Samuel was afraid to tell the vision to Eli. But Eli called Samuel and said, "Samuel, my son." He said, "Here I am." Eli said, "What was it that he told you? Do not hide it from me. May God do so to you and more also, if you hide anything from me of all that he told you." So, Samuel told him everything and hid nothing from him. Then he said, "It is the Lord; let him do what seems good to him."

—1 SAMUEL 3:1–18

I remember reading the biography of Peter Marshall, a book entitled *A Man Called Peter*, written by his wife, Catherine. Peter had an untimely death, and the book was written after he had died. The book itself was eventually turned into a movie by the same title. In the book,

Catherine tells a story about something that happened to Peter as a young man living in Scotland.

It was late at night, and Peter was walking home. He was meandering along a road he was unfamiliar with and could not see because it was so dark. While he was walking, he heard a voice: "Peter." He stopped and said, "Who is it?" There was no response. He thought he had been mistaken, and so he took a couple of more steps and once again heard the voice. Once again, Peter cried out, "Who is it?" And again, there was no response. Peter was about to take another step when he tripped, reached out his arms to catch himself, and realized that he was on the precipice of a stone quarry. One more step, and he would have fallen to his death.

Catherine then described how Peter Marshall was convinced that the voice he had heard had been the voice of God. And from that moment on, Peter was under the belief, as he was for the rest of his life, that God had called him to do something good. Peter Marshall would eventually be ordained, would become one of the more famous preachers of the first half of the twentieth century in the United States of America, and eventually become chaplain to the United States Senate. Peter Marshall lived his life convinced God had called him in a special and unique way.

A long time ago, there was a young boy by the name of Samuel. He was under the tutelage of the priest Eli. Scripture tells us that in those days, the word of the Lord was rare. No burning bushes and no earthquakes. And Samuel himself did not really know the Lord.

One evening while Samuel was lying in the temple, he heard his name called twice. *Samuel! Samuel!* Samuel gets up, convinced that Eli has called him by name. When he speaks with Eli, Eli tells him, "I have not called you by name. Go and lie down."

Samuel goes back and lies down. And again, he hears his name called, gets up once more, and heads out to report and speak with Eli. "Here I am."

Eli said, "Samuel, go lie down. I didn't call you."

The calling of Samuel's name happens yet a third time. And after the third time, Eli realizes that it is God speaking to Samuel. And so, he tells Samuel, "If you hear your name called again, say, 'Lord, here I am. Your servant is listening.'"

Samuel lies down. And God calls him by name. And Samuel responds, "Lord, here I am. Your servant is listening."

Samuel would become a great leader for the Israelite people. He would be a judge. And he would be the one who would anoint David as king, singling him out as the one God had chosen. What I appreciate very much about the passage of scripture that we read about Eli and Samuel is that Samuel is just a little boy. He is just learning his way. But he is mentored by one who has great knowledge of God; and as a result, the one who has great knowledge of God shares it with a young boy. And the boy becomes sensitive to how it is that God would speak to him. I think the same is true today.

All of us, regardless of age or station in life, I believe, are called by God—called in some particular way to do something good and great for the kingdom. Interestingly enough, there are those who have convinced themselves that God could not possibly call them. But no one is irredeemable.

And when God calls, God calls us to do that which is good for the kingdom of God and nothing else. We have all been given a particular skill set, whether we realize it or not. And I am certain that God expects us to use what it is God has given us for the greater good. Even if we don't believe we're up to the task, God would not have called us if we weren't. Perfection is not a requirement, as we all know. None of us are perfect. We are all sinful people who have made mistakes. We have done that which has failed God.

But despite our shortcomings, God chooses to use us and call us, just like God called Peter Marshall and just like God called Samuel. Now, it may not be audibly. It might be. But in some way or another, God chooses to call us. And even in our imperfections, God knows what we are capable of doing and how we can go about doing it. The Bible is filled with examples of people who have been called by God, who in one way or another appeared at least at face value not to measure up.

Moses was a murderer and had a speech impediment. He was reluctant to do that which God called him to do, to lead the Israelite people to freedom. But Moses would do it because God knew what Moses was capable of doing.

Matthew was a tax collector. That means he was despised and considered to have low character and no integrity, but he was called by Jesus to be one of his disciples. And despite his circumstances, Jesus knew what Matthew was capable of doing and the good that would reside within him.

Scripture tells us that Mary Magdalene had to have demons cast out of her by Jesus. But in all four gospel accounts, it is Mary herself who first told of Christ's resurrection. She had been a demon-possessed woman who would be freed from those demons by the power of Jesus Christ and share with the world the greatest message in human history.

And we all know about the apostle Paul, who himself was a persecutor of the early church and sought out those people who followed the one they called The Way, hoping that they would either be put to death or imprisoned. And yet Paul himself, on the road to Damascus, would be struck blind and go from being a persecutor to the greatest evangelist in the history of the church.

No matter what you have done or left undone in life, God is calling you to some specific task for the greater good of the kingdom of God. Whether you realize it or not and whether you acknowledge it or not, it is true. If God speaks to you audibly, wonderful. But I will imagine more often than not, most of us have an experience with God speaking to us in some other way.

I am of the opinion that God comes calling most of us through other people, events, circumstances, dreams, sermons ... And in the culture in which we find ourselves today, I am convinced that God is calling people to do good in a world that in so many ways has become vile.

We don't get along with each other. We squabble with one another. We belittle each other. What God wants from us is for us to do that which is good and great for the kingdom of God. And God calls us to do that and only that. It's our responsibility to listen, to look, to be intentional, and then to respond accordingly.

Jesus told an interesting parable—the parable of the talents. A man was the owner of currency talents. He gave five talents to one of his servants, two to another, and one to yet another—according to their capability, says scripture.

The one who was given five talents invested it and made five more. The one with two invested it and made two more.

And the one who was given one did absolutely nothing with what he had been given. When the wealthy man returned, he brought his servants before himself. And the one who had made five additional talents was told, "Well done, good and faithful servant." The one who doubled his talents was told, "Well done, good and faithful servant." But the rich man was very disappointed in the servant who had been given a single talent and did nothing with it. And he told him he would go to a place where there was weeping and gnashing of teeth.

The point of the parable, of course, is to take what we have been given and multiply it for the greater good. And when we do that, God is pleased. When we don't do anything with what it is God has given us, God is disappointed. Jesus told us that. Which means of course that we are born into the world for the greater good of God's kingdom. We're not here just to consume and procreate and die. We are here to do something great, to take the skill set that God has given us, that all of us have in some way or another, and utilize it for the greater good. God calls us repeatedly to do that.

The Danish philosopher Søren Kierkegaard tells a parable about the duck community. In the duck community is a duck church. And on Sunday morning, the ducks waddle into their duck church. The ducks waddle in and sit in their duck pews. The duck choir waddles into the duck choir loft, and the duck preacher waddles up to the duck pulpit. And then the duck preacher boldly proclaims, "We have been blessed by God. We have wings. We are to soar like eagles." And all the ducks shout, "Amen." And then they leave the church and waddle all the way back home.

We can hear a message, and we can shout "Amen!" But they are not just words spoken to us that are hollow. They are words that we are to integrate into our lives and to live out. We just don't waddle, we soar. We do that which God would have us to do faithfully and loyally. We do that which we are called to do as followers of Jesus Christ, listening repeatedly to what it is God would have us to do and how it is God would have us to do it.

Without exception, every one of us has been called by God to use what it is God has given us. And there is no excuse justifiable to our Lord not to take what it is God has given us and use it for those who have a need or for the greater good in some other way. All of us are called to be who God would have us to be.

I remember William Willimon talking about an occasion early in his life when he was serving a church. He would eventually become the Dean of Chapel at Duke University and a bishop in the United Methodist Church. Willimon tells how years earlier when he was serving a church, he preached about how important it was for everybody to use their skill set to do something good—that everybody has been called by God.

That week he received a phone call from a woman in his congregation who was paralyzed from the neck down. She said she wanted to do something good with the talent God had given her. Willimon said he thought, *My goodness, what can she possibly do? She's paralyzed.* But she had equipment at home that enabled her to call people on the phone. And so, she told Willimon what she would like to do. And that was that she was going to call people and remind them about church meetings, about important dates, just so they wouldn't forget to do what they had been called to do as a part of the life of the church.

Willimon describes one evening when they were having a meeting at the church. They started the meeting, and shortly afterward a man in the congregation who was on the board came in looking rather disheveled, and he sat down.

Willimon asked him, "Why were you late?" He said, "Well, I wasn't going to come to the meeting at all." "Well, why are you here?" "Because I got a call from the paralyzed woman. And she reminded me that I needed to be at the meeting. I wanted to say to her, 'I'm way too tired. It's been a long day at work.' But how do you say to someone who is paralyzed, who is using their skill set for the greater good of the kingdom, that you're too tired to do what God has called me to do? So, preacher, I'm here at this meeting after all."

We know it doesn't matter your age. Eli was an older man. Samuel was a little boy. It doesn't matter your gender. It doesn't matter whether you fully realize what you are capable of doing for God or not. If God calls you, God is going to use you, with the skills you have, to do that which is so good, to make a difference in the world for the sake of the kingdom of God.

When God calls, our answer is always yes. When God calls, our response is always to get up and do something. When God calls, we are always doing something that is good and edifying and beneficial and uplifting and encouraging.

Our world needs you right now. This country needs you right now. The kingdom of God needs you right now. Listen, God is speaking in some way to you. Somehow your responsibility and my responsibility are to listen intently, to look very closely, and to respond accordingly in faith.

When God calls, our answer is always, "Lord, here I am. Use me for the greater good."

Hallelujah. Amen.

Open Table

> Jesus entered Jericho and was passing through it. A man was there named Zacchaeus; he was a chief tax collector and was rich. He was trying to see who Jesus was, but on account of the crowd he could not, because he was short in stature. So, he ran ahead and climbed a sycamore tree to see him, because he was going to pass that way. When Jesus came to the place, he looked up and said to him, "Zacchaeus, hurry and come down, for I must stay at your house today." So, he hurried down and was happy to welcome him. All who saw it began to grumble and said, "He has gone to be the guest of one who is a sinner." Zacchaeus stood there and said to the Lord, "Look, half of my possessions, Lord, I will give to the poor, and if I have defrauded anyone of anything, I will pay back four times as much." Then Jesus said to him, "Today salvation has come to this house, because he, too, is a son of Abraham. For the Son of Man came to seek out and to save the lost."
>
> —LUKE 19:1–10

No one likes to eat alone. I imagine that's why Zacchaeus himself was so excited when Jesus invited himself into his house to share a meal. There is something about eating with other people that is a sacred and holy event.

I know soon after my mother's death I was visiting with my father, and he said, "The most difficult thing for me to do after your mother's death is to eat my meals all alone."

Have you ever been to a restaurant and seen someone sitting by herself or himself, and you had just a twinge of sadness for them? Now, they might want to be by themselves. They may be trying to get away from the kids. Who knows what's going on? But we wonder, why are they alone? It just seems like folks should not be eating by themselves.

Years ago, I heard a psychoanalyst speaking about a patient that he had, a patient who had been in a terribly abusive relationship for many years. But she had finally broken away from it. He asked her, "What was the very first thing you did when you broke away from that situation?" She said, "I drove to a restaurant parking lot. I peered into the window watching people sitting down across from each other, enjoying a meal together."

Jesus himself made a big deal out of meals. He even ate with those people whom others frowned upon. Sinners, as the scripture says, and tax collectors were hated and despised, and in the process of sharing a meal with them, Jesus did the extraordinary. He restored those people, forgave them, gave them another chance at life.

There is an occasion when Jesus met a woman at a well. She was a Samaritan woman. He struck up a conversation with her. In his culture, in that day and time, he should not have spoken to her publicly. It was forbidden for a man to speak to a woman publicly, and certainly a Samaritan woman. It was inappropriate. But in the process of offering her living water, he then went to her home, to her family. He was a Jewish man having a meal with Samaritans, considered by

Jews to be a mixed breed of people. And what Jesus did in eating with them was to make it abundantly clear that his message of grace and salvation was available to all people.

In the fourteenth chapter of the Gospel of Luke, Jesus said, "When you have a meal, a big banquet, don't invite your family and your friends and your relatives and the rich folk. But instead, go out into the street and invite those people you might not otherwise invite. The poor, the lame, the broken, the ostracized, and the alienated." And Jesus said, "If you do that, you will be blessed."

What Jesus meant by that is that there is something extraordinary that happens during a meal. And when we have a meal with other people, we discover something about them that we might not otherwise know, even those people whom we would oftentimes otherwise ignore.

No one likes to eat alone. Having a meal with other people is powerful. It's meaningful. It's important. And everyone should have a place at the table.

That's why, in the life of the church and the United Methodist Church, our table is open to all who worship there. That is, the sacrament of the Holy Communion is available to all because we believe Jesus Christ is the one who was inviting everybody. And there is always a place at the table for you, and there is always a place at the table for me. And we don't compartmentalize; we don't categorize; we don't stereotype. A place at the table is available to everyone who comes into the life of the church. We're all broken. We're all in need of a savior. And the good news is that the King of all kings invites you to his table.

In the Old Testament, David invited one to feast with him at every meal who would have come to the table staggering, struggling—a crippled man in a culture and a day in time where he would have been considered severely flawed. His name is Mephibosheth. Mephibosheth happened to be the son of Jonathan and the grandson of Saul. Saul was the king. Jonathan, Saul's son, was best friends with David; they were very close to each other, had a very powerful relationship with one another. But eventually in battle Saul was killed, as was Jonathan, his son. And David would then ascend to the throne.

And as king, one day David asked the question, "Is there anyone left in the house of Jonathan who can come and eat with me?" And he is told there is one, but he's crippled. His name is Mephibosheth. He is clearly categorized and labeled as inferior because the first thing mentioned about him is that he is crippled.

We read previous to this in 2 Samuel how Mephibosheth at the age of five was being held by a nanny, if you will, a caretaker. They found out that they might be attacked. She took Mephibosheth into her arms to flee, and while she was fleeing, she tripped and fell on him, and his legs from then on were crippled.

But King David had said, "If there is someone from the house of Jonathan, then I want to feast with him." And it is this one who is crippled, whose name is Mephibosheth. And he is invited to eat at the king's table every meal. He has a place at the table of the king, despite his physical condition. He has a place at the table, a place of honor because of who he is.

And the truth of the matter is in the life of the church, every one of us has a place at the table. Every time we gather together and worship, we have a place with each other at

the table. We are not to be compartmentalized or categorized. We have been invited by the King of all kings to have
a place at the table, a seat of honor, simply because we are
who we are. And because we believe in the powerful grace
of Almighty God, extended to all of us, God continually invites us in to be a part of all that's happening. You have a
place at the table. You don't have to be alone.

I really believe this sincerely, that Jesus Christ is inviting you and inviting me to have a place at the table once
again, our time at that sacred and holy meal. I'm not talking
just about communion, I'm talking about being together as
a church. And the one who is the greatest of all, the King
of all kings and Lord of all lords, has prepared a place for
you, a seat of honor. Your responsibility is to show up and
sit down.

I think what's important in the life of the church is that
we make it clear to people that everybody is welcome. By
the grace of God, we are not in the position to determine
who's worthy and who's not. We all need to listen to this.
There are far too many churches, even in our own denomination, who have made a determination in some way or
other about who's worthy to come and who's not. Who has
a right to do that? None of us. The One we bow before is
the One who extends an invitation. And he is the One who
lived a pristine life. He is the one whose life was unblem-
ished. And he says to everyone, "You're welcome. You have
a place at the table."

I was serving in another community, where another
church had a member of the congregation who was the
head usher, a widower who married a woman who had
been divorced many years earlier. He was informed by

the leadership of the church that he could no longer serve as usher because he married someone who had been divorced. Can you imagine that?

Our responsibility fundamentally is to be like King David, where we say, "Is there anyone out there who needs a place?" Well, there is this Mephibosheth guy, but you need to know he's flawed. He's broken. He staggers along. He's different from everybody else. And David says, "Bring it on. I've got a place for him, a seat of honor." And that's what Christ Jesus does for every single one of us.

What we have a right to do is open up the doors of the church, fling them open wide, and say, "Welcome to the church. We are glad you are here. Every one of us are broken. Every one of us is sinful. Every one of us is hypocritical. And every one of us are in need of a savior. So come on in and feast with us, worship with us, pray with us, sing with us, be one of us."

That's what it means to be the church of Jesus Christ. There are a lot of Mephibosheths in the world, and I'm one of them. There are many times when I have come into the church staggering because of my own sin that in some way has crippled me. And you know what? You know what that's like as well. Every one of us does. We're not perfect people. We don't always get it right. There are times when we make colossal errors.

But the good news is, and the world needs to hear, that we believe in a savior who loves us so much. He takes that sin away from us, and he says, "Come in. I know that's why you're here." That's why Christ died for you. He declares, "I extend grace to you—and love and mercy and forgiveness—

because I want you to be here, and I want you to be around everybody else who's just like you in one way or another."

Read 2 Samuel 9:1–13. The very last sentence says, "Now he was lame in both his feet." It says it numerous times. It talks about how Mephibosheth is welcome. King David invites him in. He's got a place of honor. And then the final line is, "Now he's lame in both his feet." You need to know he's kind of messed up. So are we all. And the good news is, we're welcome anyway. And it's our responsibility to welcome other people. We don't give a litmus test to determine whether people can fit in or who's worthy or whose life is less sinful than those other folk. We just try to be the church of Jesus Christ as we are called to be.

When I was in seminary, my first semester in seminary, I really struggled for a variety of reasons. But one of the reasons I struggled is because there were some really weird people in seminary. I mean, just strange out-of-the-ordinary people. I just didn't get it. I found out later I was actually one of them.

And I began to realize as I established relationships with these really strange people that for many of them, they knew they were strange. They knew they were different. But the reason they were in seminary is that they grew up in the life of the church where they could be just who God called them to be. They could still fit in. They still had a place of honor.

Many people in the life of the church who are in leadership positions are just a little strange.

And they're a little strange because they're allowed to be a little strange in the church. They can be a little different. They may not be the coolest, the best looking, the most popular, but they have discovered somewhere along the way the freedom that they can be who God called them to be, just as they are, without trying to fit into some kind of mold or image.

And that's what I love about the church. We're free to be who we are, fully and completely. And if we start to look too homogeneous or act too homogeneous, we need to step back and reevaluate who we are as a church. Are we doing our part to say to everyone, "You have a place at the table, please come in?"

I was serving a church that had a very powerful street ministry. And once a week we fed hundreds and hundreds of street people. The smell at times could be overwhelming.

But one of the things I greatly admired about that congregation is that many people, professional people, would give up a meal during the week and come and sit down with those street people. I would see, for example, a woman dressed beautifully, sitting next to a man who clearly hadn't bathed in weeks.

I could see a woman, carrying a luxurious, expensive purse, having a conversation and eating a meal with a woman who had all of her possessions in a little, small, tiny plastic bag. I could see a man who was a teetotaler eating with someone who was clearly an alcoholic. I remember seeing a doctor, a highly educated, prominent man in the community, enjoying a meal with a man who could not read.

And I made a determination then and there that that was what the kingdom of God really does look like, that everybody has a place at the table. Everybody belongs. Everybody is invited by the King of all kings. We all, every once in a while, stagger in here. We are all crippled by life, its mistakes, and the pain that accompanies living.

But the good news for all of us is that in every situation, at every turn, there is One who loves us unconditionally and loves us forever, who says to every one of us, "Please come and be with me. You have a seat of honor. You, indeed and forever, have a place at my table."

Hallelujah. Amen.

A Faith Built to Last

> *Hear, O Israel: The Lord is our God, the Lord alone. You shall love the Lord your God with all your heart and with all your soul and with all your might. Keep these words that I am commanding you today in your heart. Recite them to your children and talk about them when you are at home and when you are away, when you lie down and when you rise. Bind them as a sign on your hand, fix them as an emblem on your forehead, and write them on the doorposts of your house and on your gates.*
>
> —DEUTERONOMY 6:4–9

There are those things in life that are built to last, so well constructed that they have survived through the centuries. The Roman Colosseum has stood for more than two thousand years. The Great Pyramids of Egypt are approximately five thousand years old, and there are parts of the Great Wall of China that historians believe were built more than ten thousand years ago. Those are just three historical structures that were built to last, well constructed and well thought out.

But there are also those things that were not so well built, of which there are many examples. In 1981 in Kansas City, Missouri, the Hyatt Regency Hotel hosted a big celebratory party for many hundreds of people. Many walked across its fourth-floor skywalk, dancing and partying along the way, when it collapsed and fell two floors, killing 114 people because it was poorly constructed. In 2007, a bridge crossing the Mississippi River on Interstate 35 collapsed, plunging more than fifty cars into the river, where thirteen people died. It was determined that it was poorly built, though it was intended to have lasted a lot longer than it did. In 2021, in Florida, a condominium collapsed upon itself, killing ninety-eight people. Investigation later revealed that it had major cracks in it for an extended period of time that led to its destruction.

Some things built don't last because they're not well thought out. In those cases, there were no firm foundations created, no solid bases established. Scripture gives us a plan for how to live out a faith that is built to last. It is well thought out. It has a rock-solid foundation, and it is well constructed.

Moses gave it to us long ago. He told the Israelite people who would cross over into the promised land that it would be important for them always to remember and never forget that God would always be first in their lives no matter what. And that it would aways be important to teach the children about God, so it passes down from generation to generation. And that it is to be obvious—in every home, when God's people lie down and when they rise, when they're at home and when they're away—to fix it on their foreheads, place it on the doorpost of their homes, that God is first! And *that* is a faith built to last! It is rock solid in the moment. It is passed down from one generation to the next as the most important priority.

Moses said to his people, the Israelites, "Hear, O Israel, the Lord our God is our God alone. You shall love the Lord your God with all your heart, your soul, and your might." Your complete self. Remember Joshua, who would take Moses's place, his successor? Joshua said to his people, the Israelites, "Choose this day whom you will serve, but as for me and my house, we will serve the Lord." Is that a mantra in your home? Is that a statement that is transfixed on the doorpost of your house for all to see in some form or another? As New Testament people, we recognize that our relationship with God in and through Jesus Christ should be paramount.

Moses said, "God is first, teach it to your children, and show it in every circumstance all the time." For all of us who have been parents or are parents or have any kind of relationship with children, we understand how necessary and important it is to have well-rounded children. We want them to have some kind of formal education. We want them to have life experiences. We want them to be active. We want them to have good strong relationships. Those kinds of things are important, but I am telling you this: none of that ultimately matters for the long haul if Jesus Christ is not first in your home. He has to stand above all others. You want a well-rounded child? You teach your children about Jesus Christ. That is absolutely essential.

Now, there are all kinds of people who come up with all kinds of ways to rear children. But what should always be in place that enables a faith to be built to last is that Jesus Christ has to be the rock-solid foundation in your home. Period. Whether you have children at home or not makes no difference. He must be first.

There are a lot of people who get it backwards. They want well-rounded children, so they let them play soccer and baseball and participate in piano recitals and dance competitions. There is nothing wrong with any of that. But if all of that supersedes the importance of having your children in church, then you've got it backwards.

There are people who make their social life most important, and then if there is room for God, God can be worked in every now and then. That's wrong. The way it is constructed, if we follow Jesus Christ, is to place down a rock-solid foundation who is our Lord and build everything upon that. That is the central focus, and then everything else works around that.

There are times when Jesus says things that are rather disturbing, but his intent is very clear. His intent is to say, "I have to be first, and if I'm not first then you've got your priorities mixed up." Jesus says, "There will be those who come to me one day and will say to me, 'Lord, Lord,' and I will say to you, 'I don't even know who you are.'"

Jesus says that if you want a house that is rock solid, build it upon the rock of a relationship with him because all other ground is sinking sand. Jesus says, "Do not store up for yourself treasures on earth." That's where rust and moth consume. You should be building up for yourself treasures in heaven that are eternal.

If you want to leave a strong legacy for your children and your grandchildren, if you want them to know how much you love them and how important they are to you, then the best thing you can ever do is to teach them about what it means to be in relationship with Jesus Christ. He must be first. Everything else is built around that. If you want a well-rounded child, then create for them a faith that is built to last. It's critically important that we be that way in our relationship with God.

Years ago, there was a man in my congregation who was celebrating his fiftieth birthday. Already retired, he was financially well off, living in a beautiful home. He was extremely accomplished, kind of a Renaissance man, and talented in many different areas of life. His wife approached me and several of his friends, asking that for his fiftieth birthday we each write him a letter, just saying something about how much we loved him and how important he was to so many people—a letter of affirmation and encouragement. We said we'd be happy to do so.

In my letter to him I didn't write anything about all his accomplishments or his skills or talents, nor about his great personality or his appearance. You know what I said? "The most impressive thing about you is that on Sunday morning you are sitting with your family in church. That is the greatest gift you could give to your family."

Moses says that we are to make our faith so visible that it is a part of the makeup of who we are when we are at home and when we are away, when we lie down and when we rise. It has to be obvious and visible particularly to the children. Moses said that God is first, and then you teach the children, so it's passed down from generation to generation with years and years of understanding. That is so critically important to the makeup of who we are as children of God and followers of Jesus Christ. And so, as we go about living life, we remind ourselves of that, that teaching the children is of most importance.

Listen, one of the things that is most upsetting to me—and I've heard this I don't know how many times in my ministry over the years—is when parents say to me, "You haven't seen us in a while, and you haven't seen our children in a while. Our children are now twelve years old and fourteen years old. They're old enough to decide for themselves whether or not to come to church, and they've decided not to come. It's too boring."

Really? Twelve- and fourteen-year-olds get to decide that? Can you imagine leaning down and waking your little sweet angel and saying, "Honey, listen, it's Monday morning. It's time for school, but you're fourteen years old now. I'm going to let you decide for yourself whether or not you want to go to school." A fourteen-year-old doesn't make that decision. The parent makes the decision.

Can you imagine your twelve-year-old, if they came in and said, "Hey, Mom and Dad, I want you to sit down on the couch. I've got a bone to pick with you. This ten-dollars-a-week allowance ain't cutting it anymore. I want a hundred dollars a week, and I want you to open up a 401(k) account for me right now." What would you say to that child? "Are you out of your mind?" Children don't get to make critical life decisions.

You teach your children about Jesus Christ. You show it in the way you live. It is a part of the makeup of your home. If you are not doing that you are not giving your child an opportunity to build a faith that will last, that will be rock solid when they go through struggles of their own one day, when they face challenges, when they want to extend to someone out there their thanks for what has been done for them. Who are they going to do that for if there is no God in their life? That is critically important for us.

Moses talked to his community, the Israelite people. They had been wandering in the wilderness. They were soon to cross over into the promised land—the land flowing with milk and honey. But Moses said to them repeatedly in the book of Deuteronomy in a variety of ways, "Don't you forget God. Whatever you do, do not forget your God." His community that he was addressing was the Israelite people. Our community is the church of Jesus Christ. That's our community. This is where we grow in the faith. This is where we are nurturing one another. This is where we feel empowered by the Holy Spirit to be better today than we were yesterday.

John Ortberg said that generally we sin alone but we heal together. Listen to what John Mark Comer said. He said, "Our deep wounds come from relationships; and yet so does our deepest healing, because it's in relationships that we are formed and forged." We are created into somebody in the life of the church that enables us to live with an understanding that there is a God who loves us and claims us as God's very own, forever and ever. And all the joy that goes along with that. Our children deserve that.

So, Moses gave us a faith built to last. And what is that faith? It is that God is first.

You shall love the Lord your God with all your heart, all your soul, and all your might. Teach it to your children when you are at home and when you are away, when you lie down and when you rise. Well-constructed faith has a foundation in Jesus Christ that is well thought out, that is nurtured by the church itself, that grows in relationship with one another and, most importantly, in our relationship with God. If you do not have that in your home, whether you have children at home or not, I beg you to begin the process. If you don't know what to do, find a pastor you can talk to, and she or he will help and encourage you, because you are missing out.

Years ago, when my father was still active in ministry and I was in junior high school, I went through that stage in life where the church seemed so boring to me. I didn't want to be a part of it. I didn't want to have anything to do with it. I didn't want to go the youth program. I didn't want to go to Sunday school. I was never brave enough to say to my dad that I didn't want to hear his sermons anymore. I never did that, but he knew that. Growing up, the church was never optional for me. I was never given the decision to make on my own about being in the church until I went off to college.

When my kids were young, my children were very different. Rachel loved being a part of the life of the church and was very active in the youth program where all our friends were in the church. My son Sam hated it. It was boring. He didn't want to go to Sunday school, and he also never had the courage to tell his daddy he didn't want to hear his sermons. But now that they have been adults for an extended period of time, they're both very active in the church. And Sam is actually ordained in the church where he preaches every week.

You don't have to expect your children to be pastors, but you do have to expect that they're going to hear what you have to say and experience what you have to offer them. Then it is their decision about claiming it for themselves. And hopefully that will lead to a faith built to last.

Years ago, Dad told a story about when he went to a little town to be the new preacher. He attended numerous funeral services there, at his own church and at others in the area. And he noticed there was one woman in his congregation who was at every funeral he would attend. He thought to himself that she could not possibly know every single one of these people who died. So he went up to her one day and said, "I notice that every funeral I attend around town, you're there." She said, "I go to every single funeral in town whether I know them or not." Then he asked, "Why would you want to do that?" And she said, "Because it's a scary world in which we live, and the one time and the one place where I always know hope is going to be preached is at a funeral, and I cannot hear about hope enough."

See that's the great joy from being a part of the life of the church. This is where the great message of hope in Jesus Christ is found. You don't get that anywhere else. Why would you not find a way to extend that to those you love so they'll know it for themselves? It is the greatest gift you can give. If you want a faith built to last, you put God first.

If you want your children to have a faith that makes them well-rounded people—that makes them loving and caring and nurturing people, people filled with joy, people who have an inner fortitude and strength they would not otherwise have—then tell them about Jesus Christ and show it to them. That is a faith built to last.

Hallelujah. Amen.

About the Author

A native of Texas, DR. JOHN ROBBINS holds both master's and doctorate degrees from Perkins School of Theology at Southern Methodist University. He was ordained as an elder in 1992 and has served United Methodist congregations across Texas and Arkansas for nearly four decades.

Dr. Robbins currently serves as senior pastor of Pulaski Heights United Methodist Church in Little Rock, Arkansas, which is known for its far-reaching online and broadcast ministry. John and his wife, Susan, have two children and five grandchildren.